The
Mysteries of Research

Second Edition

Sharron Cohen

Alleyside Press

Fort Atkinson, Wisconsin

Published by Alleyside Press, an imprint of
Highsmith Press LLC
W5527 Highway 106
P.O. Box 800
Fort Atkinson, Wisconsin 53538-0800

1-800-558-2110

Cover by Frank Neu

The paper used in this publication meets the minimum requirements of American National Standard for Information Science — Permanence of Paper for Printed Library Material. ANSI/NISO Z39.48-1992.

Library of Congress Cataloging-in-Publication Data

Cohen, Sharron.

    The mysteries of research / Sharron Cohen. – 2nd ed.
       p.   cm.
   ISBN 0-917846-76-1 (paper : alk. paper)
   1. Reference books–Problems, exercises, etc. 2. Educational games. 3. Mystery games. I. Title.
  Z711.C429 1996
  028.7' 076–dc20   95-43103

ISBN 0-917846-76-1

Contents

To the Librarian or Teacher

Students are often taught how to find information, but they don't always know how to decide for themselves what information to look up. Nor do they always have a use for the information (beyond writing it down and handing it in to the teacher) after they have found it. The program contained in *The Mysteries of Research* is designed to bridge the gap between reference skills and thinking skills by giving students a set of problems whose solutions require both research and logical thought.

Ideally, the mysteries in this book will be used by students who have already had some instruction in the use of reference books. If some students have not, you should spend a few preliminary sessions introducing them to the reference sources. The appendix to this book contains reference tests (with answer keys) that you can use to assess students' abilities to choose access words and appropriate reference books.

A sample mystery ("The Mystery of the Leaping Lepidopterans") is also included. Working through the sample mystery as a class, you can show students how to research the necessary facts and then how to use the clues to reach a logical conclusion.

Deciding what to look up is sometimes more difficult for students than doing the research itself. If that is the case, you might want to underline some or all of the facts that require checking on the students' worksheets before they start.

The mysteries can be solved by individuals or by groups of students working together. The mysteries require one to three hours to solve, depending on the category of the mystery—easy, intermediate, or difficult—and the abilities of the students. Students can report their findings to you verbally or hand in a written solution. (A sample Detective's Report, appropriate to use for written solutions, is included in the next section of this book.)

This book contains three categories of mysteries. In the easy mysteries, the plots are relatively simple and every statement made by the guilty parties is a lie. In the intermediate mysteries, not all statements made by the guilty parties are incorrect and the facts to be checked are woven into the mysteries in a less obvious way. Difficult mysteries provide a greater number of facts to be checked, often in lengthier reference book entries. In addition, the difficult mysteries require students to go beyond the obvious, either in pursuing a line of research or in drawing logical conclusions. But, even within categories, some mysteries are more difficult than others.

Regardless of the category of the mystery, one premise always holds true: The suspect or suspects who lie or give inaccurate information are guilty.

The mysteries were written and solved using a very basic set of reference sources (*The World Book Encyclopedia,* 1994 edition, *The Guinness Book of Records,* 1994 edition, *Webster's New Collegiate Dictionary, The World Almanac and Book of Facts, World Book Atlas, Rand McNally Universal World Atlas,* and the *Hammond/Simon & Schuster World Atlas*) but you should not limit your students to these sources if your library has a greater selection. Students can use identification guides, biographical dictionaries, the card catalog, and books on the general circulation shelves to find information.

Some information may be difficult or even impossible to find. Although your students may use (1) different reference sources, from those used in writing and solving the mysteries in this book or (2) more recent editions of the reference sources in which some information may have been eliminated, they should still be able to solve the mysteries. Every suspect's profile contains several facts to be checked, at least one of which will appear in a variety of reference sources. Students should be cautioned that the failure to find a fact in the reference sources does not prove a suspect's guilt.

Research Detective's Starter Kit

Memorandum to Research Recruits

To: Research Bureau Detective Recruits

From: Research Bureau Chief

Re: An Introduction to the Bureau

Welcome to the Research Bureau. As detective recruits, you are part of an elite corps dedicated to truth, justice, and clear thinking.

Very soon, you will be assigned your first case, which consist of a description of a crime and profiles of four suspects, In your first and all other cases, one or more of the suspects will lie to you. Any suspect who lies is guilty of the crime committed, and it is up to you to uncover evidence against him or her. Using the reference books in your classroom or library, you will determine the following facts:

- which suspects are telling the truth,
- which suspect or suspects are lying and therefore guilty,
- how the crime was committed,
- why the crime was committed, and
- if something was stolen, where it can be found.

Please review the attached Golden Rules for Research Detectives before starting to work on your first case.

Good luck to each of you.

Attachment: Golden Rules for Research Detectives

Golden Rules for Research Detectives

1. A research bureau detective plans carefully before beginning a search.

Before you do anything else, read through the whole case to get a general idea of what crime has been committed and who the suspects are. Then, go back and read through the mystery again, this time underlining everything you think you should look up. Names of the suspects are fictitious (made up), but you should check all dates and look up the meanings of words you do not know.

2. A research bureau detective is efficient.

Take a few minutes to look over the words and facts you've underlined. Which items require you to use a dictionary? Put a D above them. Mark the items that require you to use an atlas with an AT, those that require you to use an encyclopedia with an E, those that require you to use an almanac with an ALM, and those that require you to use the *Guinness Book of World Records* with a G.

When you go to the dictionary, look up all the words for which you need a dictionary. Note the meanings of those words on your workpaper. Then, move on to the atlas, and do the same. Do the same for each reference book that you use. That way you won't lose valuable time rushing back and forth from one book to another.

3. A research bureau detective does not leap to conclusions.

Do not substitute guesswork for research. Look up information even if you think you already know it. You may find that you didn't know it after all.

Do not stop researching a suspect after you have caught him or her in one lie. Other mistakes by the same suspect may give you valuable clues on how and why the crime was committed.

4. A research bureau detective is careful.

When you have finished using a reference book, return it to the shelf and the spot where you found it. And, in a library book, never underline the information you are looking for. If you must use something to keep track of your place, use a small ruler or a piece of paper.

5. A research bureau detective thinks clearly.

Suspects who lie are guilty. Suspects who do not lie are innocent. After your research has revealed which suspects have lied and which have not, reread the mystery, putting together all the facts and statements until you have figured out why and how the crime was committed and if something was stolen, where it is.

How to Use Reference Books

Years ago, you probably learned how to use reference books by using a reference book that is in most of the homes in America–the telephone book.

Maybe it surprises you to have a telephone book referred to as a reference book. People usually think of reference books as huge, expensive volumes that librarians hover over, not as paperback books the telephone company gives away for free. However, a reference book is simply a book that contains useful information, and nothing could be more useful than a book that contains the addresses and telephone numbers of almost everyone in your hometown.

It's as easy as ABC

The telephone book contains an alphabetical listing of names. That means that every person whose last name begins with the letter A is listed before every person whose last name begins with the letter B, and so on. A person whose last name is "Abell" is listed before one whose last name is "Adams" (look at the second letter of the names), and "Atkins" comes before "Atkinson." When people have the same last name, the book continues to list them in alphabetical order by their first names, so "Allen, Anthony" comes before "Allen, Judith."

The encyclopedia also contains an alphabetical listing—of both names and other information. Like the telephone book, it lists people in alphabetical order by their last names. "Kennedy, John F." comes before "Washington, George." Kennedy, John F." comes after "Kennedy, Benjamin" and before "Kennedy, William" in the encyclopedia because J (for John) comes after B (for Benjamin) and before W (for William) in the alphabet.

Let's go back to the telephone book for a minute. You look up people by their last names, but you wouldn't look up the name of The Rock 'n' Roll Music Store under "Store, The Rock 'n' Roll Music," although Store is the last word in the name. You would look it up under the first word of its title, "Rock." (The words "The" and "A" are ignored when they come first in a title.)

Book titles, events, places, and objects are listed exactly the same way in an encyclopedia—by the first word of their title. (Remember to ignore The's and A's if they are the first words.) "The French and Indian Wars" comes before "Kennedy, John F." in the encyclopedia because F comes before K in the alphabet. "Georgia" comes before "Juvenile Delinquency" for the same reason.

Like a telephone book and an encyclopedia, a dictionary also contains alphabetical listings of information, this time on words. But, what about an atlas? An atlas usually groups countries together according to which continent they are on. "France" follows the "Netherlands" and comes before "Spain" and "Portugal," in no particular alphabetical order. Almanacs and the *Guinness Book of World Records* do not follow alphabetical order either.

Don't panic! A reference book that is not organized alphabetically always has an index. The index is usually found at the end of the book and is alphabetically arranged just like the telephone book. The index gives you the page number where the information can be found in the book.

Although encyclopedias are arranged alphabetically, they also have an index, usually in a separate volume. An index in an encyclopedia is useful for two reasons:

1. It tells you every place in the encyclopedia where the person or event you are researching is mentioned. For instance, George Washington is mentioned in 26 separate places in the 1994 edition of *The World Book Encyclopedia.*

2. The index tells you where to look for people, places, or events that do not have their own listing in the encyclopedia. For instance, you cannot find "Major Richard I. Bong" in *The World Book Encyclopedia* unless you use the index. The index tells you that "Bong, Richard I." is mentioned in a listing titled "War Aces" in Volume W.

Reference books shorthand

Because reference books have to pack a lot of information into a limited amount of space, they often use a form of shorthand. Instead of listing, "John Tyler was born in 1790 and died in 1862," the encyclopedia might indicate "Tyler, John (1790-1862)." Sometimes the information is written like

this: "b. 1790 d. 1862." The "b." stands for date of birth and the "d." stands for date of death. Be careful, though. In *The World Almanac and Book of Facts,* John Tyler's name is followed by these dates: 1841–1845. Knowing that he was president of the United States, you should be able to figure out that the dates cover his term as president.

Taking advantage of shortcuts

When an encyclopedia entry is long, the publishers often include a sidebar—a box containing the most important dates and information. For instance, suppose you are looking for information about George Washington. The article on George Washington in the 1994 edition of *The World Book Encyclopedia* is nineteen pages long, but there are several sidebars, one of which lists the most important events in his life. Sometimes the information in the sidebars is enough to answer your questions.

At other times, the information in the sidebars is insufficient. Suppose you want to know *how* George Washington died. You could read through the entire nineteen pages, or you could be logical about the search. Because a person's death comes at the end of his of her life, it is logical to guess that information about his of her death would come at the end of the article. Start your reading a paragraph or two from the end of the article, and see if you can find the needed information there.

There is another way to read quickly through a long encyclopedia entry. Read only the bold (or very dark) print (headings and subheadings) until you find the time, for example, in George Washington's life for which you are looking. Halfway through *The World Book Encyclopedia* entry on George Washington, you might find the heading "First in War (1775–1783)," followed by the subheadings "Symbol of Independence," "Discouragement," "The Army," "Shortage of Supplies," "Winning the War," and "Turning Down a Crown." By reading the headings and subheadings, you have scanned the entire Revolutionary War in seven short phrases.

If you continue to scan through the entry on George Washington, you might find the heading "First in the Hearts of his Countrymen (1797–1799)," followed by the subheading "Death." By reading the paragraphs that follow that subheading, you would learn the details of George Washington's death.

Where to Look for Information

Almanac

Almanacs are good places to look for lists and statistics. They contain information about Academy Award, Pulitzer Prize, Nobel Prize, and Olympic Game Winners; U.S. holidays; inventors and their inventions; mayors of major U.S. cities; and major fires, hurricanes, volcanic eruptions and other disasters. They also contain pictures of the flags of every country, short biographies on the U.S. presidents, descriptions of the planets in our solar system, and information about the 50 U.S. states and major U.S. cities.

Because almanacs contain so much information on so many different topics, they are a logical place to turn when you cannot find information in any other reference source.

The index is in the front of most almanacs.

Atlas

Atlases contain maps of the United States and the world. Most atlases include information on the number of people who live in every city listed and a mileage scale that can help you determine the distance between any two points on a map. Some atlases have a complete index in the back of the book, but other atlases have only a general index that refers you to a more detailed index beside each map. (For example, you can find Burlington, Iowa, in the index of some atlases. In other atlases, you can find only Iowa listed in the index, but a more detailed index beside the map of Iowa would list the city of Burlington.)

Atlases give map coordinates for each place listed, usually as a number and a letter, like E3. To locate that place on the map, find the letters and numbers at the top and on the side of the page, respectively. Run one finger down the page from the E, and another finger across the page from the 3. The area where your fingers touch is E3.

Biographical dictionary

Biographical dictionaries contain information about famous people. Entries here are shorter than those in an encyclopedia. People are listed alphabetically by their last names, just as they are in a telephone book.

Dictionary

Dictionaries contain the meanings of words and a guide to their pronunciation. Words are listed alphabetically.

Encyclopedia

Encyclopedias contain information about people, places, and events. Information is arranged alphabetically, and most encyclopedias have an index (usually the last volume of the set). The index is useful for locating information that does not have its own listing in one of the main encyclopedia volumes.

Guinness Book of World Records

Use the *Guinness Book of World Records* for information about world records and superlatives (anything that is the best, biggest, smallest, oldest, youngest, or "most" something in any category). Because some of the information is so outrageous, this book is a lot of fun to read.

Reference books at a glance

Here is a quick and easy guide to the kinds of information that you will find in the six commonly used reference books just discussed.

Almanac–Lists and statistics

Atlas–maps

Biographical Dictionary–People

Dictionary–Words

Encyclopedia–People, places, and events

Guinness Book of World Records–World records and superlatives

Detective's Report

(For each suspect, give reasons for your decision on guilt or innocence.)

Title of Mystery:

Suspect 1

Age_____   Guilty_____   Innocent_____

Suspect 2

Age_____   Guilty_____   Innocent_____

Suspect 3

Age_____   Guilty_____   Innocent_____

Suspect 4

Age_____   Guilty_____   Innocent_____

How was the crime committed?

Why was the crime committed?

If something was stolen, where is it?

The Mystery of the Leaping Lepidopterans

The Crime

On May 13, Professor Horace Criggle notified the Research Bureau that his valuable pupa collection had disappeared from his home. "I kept it in here," he explained, leading the detectives into his study. "It was here this morning, but when I returned from the university this evening, it was gone. Poof! Six months of my lepidopteran research out the window."

Despite the warmth of the day, all the windows in the study were shut and locked. Professor Criggle explained that his wife insisted on having the rest of the windows in the house open during the day but that the maids were always told to keep the study windows shut for security reasons.

The room had been vacuumed and dusted that day, but there were a few bits of brown detritus in the corner of the shelf where the pupa collection had been kept.

The Problem

What happened to the pupa collection?

The Suspects

Suspect 1: Louise Criggle

Louise Criggle, Professor Criggle's wife was born in Cape May, on the southern tip of New Jersey, the year that Nicolas Mordvinoff won the Caldecott Medal for *Finders Keepers*.

She does not share her husband's fondness for lepidopterans. "It could be worse," she admitted. "When we were first married, he was involved in arachnid research. He kept a Goliath bird-eating spider, which is the largest spider on earth, in a cage in the dining room. The ghastly thing kept watching our parakeet. When I found out that arachnids also include scorpions and ticks, I made him change to lepidopteran research. Not that they're much better. A bug is a bug, no matter what you call it, and I can't abide the idea of having bugs in my house."

Louise Criggle's alibi: "I was at a meeting of my horticultural club all morning and returned home just in time to watch 'Wheel of Fortune' on the television in my third-floor bedroom. I remember that because I liked the chartreuse dress Vanna White was wearing and called my dressmaker to see if she could make me one just like it. I spent the rest of the day trying to hire domestic help because I fired our cook and maid last week."

Suspect 2: Toni-Lee Criggle

Toni-Lee Criggle, Professor Criggle's daughter, was born in Soufriere, St. Lucia, where her father was making a collection of lepidopterans of the Lesser Antilles. She was born the year that Henry Kissinger won the Nobel Peace Prize. Despite her parents' hope that she would be a cellist, Toni-Lee dropped out of the conservatory to become a chanteuse.

"I'm currently performing in a Richard Rodgers revue at a local nightclub," she told us. "My favorite song is 'The Lady is a Tramp,' but my boyfriend Raymond prefers 'Falling in Love with Love.' He's such a romantic. I believe that he's a descendant of Johann Sebastian Bach," she confided in us. "Raymond says there's no genealogical proof, but he could be. After all, the composer had twenty children."

Toni-Lee does not mind lepidopterans. It's her father she despises. "He cares more about insects than he does about people. Just look at what he did to poor Raymond. I'm glad somebody stole his creepy chrysalises, but don't look at me. I didn't do it."

Toni-Lee Criggle's alibi: "I slept most of the morning, then got up and manicured my fingernails. At 4 P.M. I had a clandestine rendezvous with Raymond Feenbothom. We met at a sidewalk cafe, where I ordered the salmagundi and a cherry Coke."

Suspect 3: Raymond Bach Feenbothom

Raymond Bach Feenbothom, Professor Criggle's former assistant, was born in Regensburg, Germany, on the banks of the Danube River. He was born the year that Judy Garland died.

"I used to keep records on the migration routes of monarch butterflies from Canada to Mexico," Raymond told us. "But I was fired when I refused to asphyxiate monarch imagos for Professor Criggle's collection. I'm now pursuing a career as a bibliopole."

Raymond Feenbothom's alibi: "I spent all day with a customer who was looking for a copy of the *Book of Changes*, which is also known as the *I Ching*. At 4P.M. I met Toni-Lee Criggle at a sidewalk cafe. I ordered fettucine and mocha frappe."

Suspect 4: Charles C. Charles

Charles C. Charles, the Criggles' butler, was born in the capital of city of Louisiana the year that Queen Victoria of England was born.

Because he was born and raised in New Orleans, he is a wonderful cook. "Good thing, too," he told us resentfully. "Ever since the cook and maid were fired I've had to do everything around here—cook, dust, vacuum, open all the windows to air the house out, and polish the silver. And, the Criggles want it all done to perfection. Mrs. Criggles fired the cook for making a lumpy haggis, and the maid was sent packing because she refused to walk the corgi. Who can blame her? That dog is too big for one tiny slip of a girl to manage all alone. I much prefer the collie breed, which originated in Ireland in the 1300s, but Mrs. Criggle dotes on that spoiled corgi. Don't get me wrong, though," Charles C. Charles hastened to add, "I need this job, and I'd do anything not to lose it."

Charles C. Charles' alibi: "I was polishing the silver most of the day, stopping only long enough to watch 'Wheel of Fortune' on the television set in the study. I didn't notice if the lepidopterans were still there because I was too busy wondering how Vanna White could breathe in the skintight red dress she was wearing."

The Solution

The butler did it, but he didn't mean to. The poor man was so overworked that he forgot that the windows in the study were not supposed to be opened. It was a warm May day, and the pupae did what pupae do in the spring: they hatched and flew away through the open study windows.

When Charles C. Charles went into the study to watch "Wheel of Fortune," he saw that the pupae were gone, and he knew he'd probably be fired. Because he didn't want to lose his job, he decided to cover up the incident by vacuuming the remains of the cocoons off the shelf. He was so busy doing that, he didn't notice the color of the dress Vanna White was wearing.

Information about the suspects

Suspect 1—Mrs. Louise Criggle

Cape May is on the southern tip of New Jersey.

Nicolas Mordvinoff won the Caldecott Medal for *Finders Keepers* in 1952.

The Goliath bird-eating spider is the largest spider in the world.

Spiders, scorpions and ticks are all arachnids.

Suspect 2—Toni-Lee Criggle

Soufriere, St. Lucia, is in the Lesser Antilles.

Henry Kissinger won the Nobel Peace Prize in 1973.

Richard Rodgers wrote both "The Lady Is a Tramp" and "Falling in Love with Love."

The composer Johann Sebastian Bach had twenty children.

Suspect 3—Raymond Bach Feenbothom

Regensburg, Germany, is on the banks of the Danube River.

Judy Garland died in 1969.

Monarch butterflies migrate from Canada to Mexico.

The *Book of Changes* is also known as the *I Ching*.

Suspect 4—Charles C. Charles

Baton Rouge, not New Orleans, is the capital of Louisiana.

Queen Victoria of England was born in 1819.

Although they are strong, corgis are small dogs.

The collie originated in Scotland, probably in the 1600s.

Easy
Mysteries

The Mystery of the Burned Bunny Books

The Crime

The Daffodil Publishing Company has rewritten the Beatrix Potter books to make them "more relevant to today's children." Not only have they changed Beatrix Potter's words, they've also taken out Beatrix Potter's lovely illustrations and replaced them with photographs of puppets. But, that's not the crime we've been asked to investigate.

Five hundred thousand copies of the new, revised *The Tale of Peter Rabbit* were destroyed in a fire at the Daffodil Publishing Company warehouse. Police found an empty gasoline can in the alley behind the warehouse, and they have concluded that the fire was a case of arson.

The Problem

Who set fire to the warehouse?

The Suspects

Suspect 1: Millicent Fenwick

Millicent Fenwick, the president of the Beatrix Potter Fan Club, was born in Spartanburg, which is west of Rock Hill, South Carolina, the year that Robert McCloskey won the Caldecott Medal for *Time of Wonder*.

"Beatrix Potter was the daughter of wealthy Londoners," Millicent Fenwick told us. "But her happiest moments were spent in the Lake District of northern England. Her illustrations for *The Tale of Peter Rabbit*, which was first published in 1902, were based on the landscapes of her beloved Lake District."

"Now this dreadful publisher has removed all the lovely pastoral illustrations," she lamented. "He claims they were too bland to hold a child's attention. He has deleted the fact that Peter Rabbit's father was baked in a pie by Mrs. MacGregor because that was too disturbing and violent for a child's psyche. Bosh and hogwash! He has taken a brilliantly written book and turned it into pure garbage! Those books were trash before they burned. The fire didn't make them any more so."

Millicent Fenwick's alibi: "I was at home rereading *The Tale of Mrs. Tiggy-Winkle*, the original version," she stressed, "the way Beatrix Potter wrote it."

Suspect 2: Horace Horton

Horace Horton, the publisher of the rewritten version of *The Tale of Peter Rabbit*, was born in Ephrata, Washington, on the coast of the Pacific Ocean, the same year that William Randolph Hearst was born.

"That Fenwick woman was a real pain. She even accused me of making Peter Rabbit look like a hare, "Horace Horton told us.

"Of course he looks like a hare! There aren't any differences between a rabbit and a hare. Anyway, my Peter Rabbit was modeled after a jack rabbit. That should tell you how careful I was about the truth."

"These things happen," he shrugged philosophically when we asked him about the fire. "The Lord gives and then the Lord takes away. What can I say? The warehouse was an old building that needed renovation. Luckily, I had just insured it for $5 million. The revised version of *The Tale of Peter Rabbit* wasn't selling very well, anyway. Kids don't relate to rabbits anymore. They'd rather read about bellicose mutated adolescent reptiles."

Horace Horton's alibi: "I was having a meeting with a writer. Well, he's not exactly a writer. He's a 'concept man' who has a really great idea about marketing a battery-operated book. Kids won't have to learn to read now. It'll save everyone a lot of time."

Suspect 3: Andrew Random, III

Andrew Random, III, the president of the International Writer's Guild, was born in Lake Havasu City, Arizona, near the Arizona-California border, the year that Ernest Hemingway died.

Andrew Random was so infuriated by the rewritten edition of *The Tale of Peter Rabbit* that he sued the Daffodil Publishing Company, claiming that they were selling a "vile perversion of a deceased author's work." "No one has a right to change an author's words, even after the author is dead and gone," Andrew Random insisted. "If Horace Horton is allowed to do this, what will be next? Will he rewrite Laura Ingalls Wilder's *Farmer Boy* because the majority of children in the United States do not live on farms? Will he change Clement Clark Moore's *'Twas the Night Before Christmas* because modern children don't know what a sugarplum is?" Andrew Random was eloquent, but Horace Horton won the lawsuit.

Andrew Random's alibi: "I was with my lawyer, trying to think of a way to stop that hideous little book from being distributed."

Suspect 4: Hilary Horton

Hilary Horton, the son and heir of Horace Horton, was born in Clearwater, which is on the west coast of Florida, the year that *One Flew Over the Cuckoo's Nest* won the Academy Award for best motion picture.

Hilary was very nervous when he talked with us. "I've got a few phobias," he admitted. "Zoophobia, especially when it comes to cats. That's a whole phobia by itself—ailurophobia. Hydrophobia and pyrophobia—fear of water and fire—and claustrophobia. This is a very small room we're in," he complained as sweat ran down his forehead. "I'm having a hard time breathing. Do you think we could go outside?"

Hilary Horton's alibi: "I wasn't in the warehouse the night of the fire," he admitted guiltily. "I saw a black cat sitting on the windowsill, and I took off in a panic. I must have run for half an hour before I calmed down enough to go back." Because Hilary had such a hard time finding a job elsewhere, Horace Horton gave him the job of night watchman at the Daffodil Publishing Company warehouse.

The Solution

Children are smarter than Horace Horton expected them to be. They didn't want the new, watered-down "relevant" version of *The Tale of Peter Rabbit*, so the books sat in the warehouse gathering dust and losing money. As soon as Horace Horton insured the warehouse fully, he spilled a can of gasoline and struck a match. To get his son out of the building, he placed a black cat on the windowsill before igniting the warehouse, but the fact that he would scare his son so badly just shows that he is the kind of man who would rewrite Beatrix Potter's books.

Information about the suspects

Suspect 1—Millicent Fenwick

Spartanburg, South Carolina, is west of Rock Hill, South Carolina.

Robert McCloskey won the Caldecott Medal for *Time of Wonder* in 1958.

Beatrix Potter was the daughter of wealthy Londoners.

Beatrix Potter's illustrations were based on the landscapes of the Lake District of northern England.

The Tale of Peter Rabbit was first published in 1902.

Peter Rabbit's father was baked in a pie by Mrs. MacGregor.

Beatrix Potter also wrote *The Tale of Mrs. Tiggy-Winkle*.

Suspect 2—Horace Horton

Ephrata, Washington, is not on the coast of the Pacific Ocean.

William Randolph Hearst was born in 1863.

Rabbits tend to be a little smaller and have shorter ears than hares.

Newborn rabbits are blind, have no fur, and cannot move around. Newborn hares can see, have fine fur, and can hop about several hours after birth.

Jack rabbits are hares.

Suspect 3—Andrew Random, III

Lake Havasu City, Arizona, is near the Arizona-California border.

Ernest Hemingway died in 1961.

Laura Ingalls Wilder wrote *Farmer Boy*.

Clement Clark Moore wrote *An Account of a Visit from St. Nicholas*, which is often referred to as *'Twas the Night Before Christmas*.

Suspect 4—Hilary Horton

Clearwater is on the west coast of Florida.

One Flew Over the Cuckoo's Nest won the Academy Award for best motion picture in 1975.

Zoophobia is an intense fear of animals.

Ailurophia is an intense fear of cats.

Hydrophobia is an intense fear of water.

Pyrophobia is an intense fear of fire.

Claustrophobia is an intense fear of being in an enclosed or confined space.

The Mystery of the Disintegrating Dress

The Crime

It was Buffy Cutshrink's big chance for success. She had been invited to join clothing designers from all over the world in an all-day fashion show at Rockefeller Plaza in New York City. Buffy's neophyte company didn't have enough money to advertise in fashion magazines, but this show would allow her to display her company's designs next to those of the world's most influential designers. She and her employees rushed to complete a wedding gown.

"A floor-length acrylic bridal gown edged with synthetic fur at the cuffs and hemline, designed by Clorinda Hathaway of the Cutshrink Fashion Company," the announcer told the audience as the model glided down the runway. Few photographers bothered to raise their cameras until the model inadvertently stepped on the hem and the waistline of the wedding gown ripped apart. As the model reached down to keep the skirt from falling, her sleeve slid down her forearm and landed on the floor.

Buffy Cutshrink fainted. Photographers leaped up to record the unexpected spectacle. In the chaos that followed, very little of the dress remained intact. Fortunately, the model was wearing a demure muslin slip.

The Problem

Who loosened the seams of the wedding gown?

The Suspects

Suspect 1: Countess Alexandria von Vogue

Countess Alexandria von Vogue, doyenne of the von Vogue Fashion Company, was born in Basildon, a short distance east of London, England, the year that the Duke of Windsor married Wallis Warfield Simpson.

"I started the von Vogue Fashion Company years ago when my husband, the earl, lost his ancestral lands and fortune," Countess von Vogue told us. "But, I continued to call myself countess. An earl's wife is entitled to that title, and it is good for business. One of my very first customers was the wife of King George VI of England, whose maiden name was Lady Elizabeth Bowes-Lyon."

"I overheard that vulgar Cutshrink woman tell a reporter that her company's wedding gown was more trendy than the one my company had designed," the countess continued haughtily. "I certainly hope so! My company prides itself on producing clothes that are timeless, not faddish."

Countess Alexandria von Vogue's alibi: "I was in my model's dressing room. I could have slipped in and weakened the seams of her dresses, but I didn't. The lioness has no need to swat at flies."

Suspect 2: Clorinda Hathaway

Clorinda Hathaway, designer for the Cutshrink Fashion Company, was born in Riviere-du-Loup, Quebec, on the banks of the Saint Lawrence River, the year that *My Fair Lady* won the Academy Award for best motion picture.

"Don't ask me about that dress! I hate that dress!" Clorinda responded to our questions. "Do you think I would design some-thing as cliched and boring as that wedding gown? No! My design called for the gown to be made from the finest grade of silk, which is produced by the Asian Bombyx mori moth, edged with sable. But, Buffy Cutshrink's husband objected to the cost, so Buffy substituted acrylic for the silk and fake fur for the sable. Acrylic!" Clorinda cried. "Do you know what acrylic is made from? It's made from petroleum! What kind of fashion statement is a woman mak-ing when she wears a petroleum product on her wedding day?"

Clorinda Hathaway's alibi: "I was running back and forth between the Cutshrink dressing room and the table at the outdoor cafe where Buffy and her husband George were going over the latest cost figures for the company. When I begged Buffy to with-draw the gown from the show, Buffy's cheapskate husband suggested that I quit so they could hire a designer whose ideas were more compatible with the company's budget. I begged the Cutshrink's model, Tandoori, not to wear the dress in the show, but she just shrugged and said she needed the job."

Suspect 3: George Cutshrink

George Cutshrink, Buffy Cutshrink's hus-band, was born in Hanging Rock, Ohio, near the southern border of the state, the year that Andrew William Mellon died.

George Cutshrink, a self-made millionaire, bankrolled his wife's fashion company with the understanding that if it didn't make a profit within three years, she would "give up this career woman nonsense and come home where she belonged."

"The fashion profession is too fickle for my tastes," George Cutshrink admitted. "One year hems are at the knee and primary colors are the rage, the next year hems are halfway to the ankle and everyone wants pastels. If you guess wrong, you're out of luck and out of dough.

"Do you want to know what I consider a good investment?" George Cutshrink whispered conspiratorially, "Cattle. Buy yourself some Brahman or Hereford cattle for the meat market or some Holstein-Friesian and Guernsey cows for the milk market. If they die on you, you can sell their skin for leather."

George Cutshrink's alibi: "I was at the outdoor cafe with Buffy most of the day going over the Cutshrink Fashion Company's books and advising her on how to cut down on her expenses. I left the table a few times to call my stockbroker, but I didn't go anywhere near the Cutshrink dressing room."

Suspect 4: Tandoori

Tandoori, the Cutshrink model, was born in Palermo, Italy, on the Italian Riviera, the year that Norma Smallwood won the Miss America Contest.

"From the first, I do not like the dress," Tandoori told us sulkily. "I think to myself, 'I will not get attention from a single paparazzo. Tandoori will not get the same attention as the von Vogue model.' That is the way of it, to be unfair."

"Someone cuts the seams to accomplish revenge on Mrs. Cutshrink. The dress falls apart, one, two, three, and I am standing there in only my lingerie. A paparazzo takes a picture, then another and another. I am on the front page of all the newspapers. A Hollywood producer calls to ask me to take a screen test, and someday I am as famous as the American movie star, George Bryan Brummell, before he died in a car crash. I tell the Cutshrinks, 'Ha! I am Tandoori, and I do not need your boring dresses to make me a famous star.' Unfair has been stood on its head now, has it not?"

Tandoori's alibi: "I am here and there, visiting with other models and comparing what we are to wear in the fashion show. Then, I return to my dressing room to clip and manicure my nails."

The Solution

Tandoori visited the other models in the show and looked over the creations they were to model. They were all more sensational than the Cutshrink Fashion Company's entry in the fashion show. Tandoori knew that no one would look at her twice in the undistinguished creation she was going to wear. The photographers would not take her picture.

Tandoori thought about the situation while she clipped and filed her nails. Then, deciding to "stand unfair on its head," as Tandoori would no doubt put it, she used the fingernail clippers and yanked the waistline loose. A turn in the right direction ripped the loosened sleeve. A wriggle here and a wriggle there managed to unhinge the entire dress and get her all the attention any picture-happy model could desire.

Information about the suspects

Suspect 1—Countess Alexandria von Vogue

Basildon is a short distance east of London, England.

The Duke of Windsor married Wallis Warfield Simpson in 1937.

An earl's wife is called a countess.

Lady Elizabeth Bowes-Lyon was the maiden name of the wife of King George VI of England.

Suspect 2—Clorinda Hathaway

Riviere-du-Loup, Quebec, is on the banks of St. Lawrence River.

My Fair Lady won the Academy Award for best motion picture in 1964.

The finest grade of silk is produced by the Asian Bombyx mori moth.

Acrylic is made from petroleum.

Suspect 3—George Cutshrink

Hanging Rock, Ohio, is near the southern border of the state.

Andrew William Mellon died in 1937.

Brahmans and Herefords are meat cattle.

Hosthein-Friesians and Guernseys are milk cattle.

Suspect 4—Tandoori

Palermo is in Sicily, not on the Italian Riviera.

Norma Smallwood won the Miss America Contest in 1926.

George Bryan Brummell (Beau Brummell) was English, not American. He died in 1840, before the first movies were ever made.

Beau Brummell died in a French mental institution, not in a car crash.

The Mystery of the Lost Library Loot

The Crime

A box of new books has been stolen from the school library. "When they arrived yesterday morning I put them over there," the librarian told us, pointing to the worktable in the back of the library. "Before I can put new books on the shelves, I have to stamp them with the name of the school, cover them with book jackets, glue card pockets in the back, and make out catalog cards for each book."

"I didn't have time to do that yesterday because I was in the school lobby all day putting up an exhibit for National Library Week."

The Problem

Who stole the library books?

The Suspects

Suspect 1: Olive Shushingham

Olive Shushingham, the school's librarian, was born in Cape Girardeau, Missouri, right beside the Missouri River, the same year that Agatha Christie was born.

"You have no idea what I have put up with in this library," Miss Shushingham complained. "As soon as I get the shelves all neat and tidy, hordes of little barbarians rush in to pull books out and drop them on the floor. They don't care about the Dewey Decimal Classification System that the famous judge, Merwin Dewey, developed. They take art books out of the 900s and stick them in with the science books in the 400s. They paw at the clean, white pages with their dirty little hands. They rip the pages and tear the bindings. Now, someone has actually stolen a box of books!"

"Sometimes I think that children don't deserve books. Books should be locked in the library closet and shown only to the few polite students who are capable of appreciating them."

Olive Shushingham's alibi: "I was in the lobby all day preparing an exhibit for National Library Week. I was putting up pictures of Katherine Paterson, the 1992 winner of the Newbery Medal. I returned to the library at the end of the day to get my coat and purse, but I was in such a hurry I didn't notice if the books were still on the table. They certainly weren't there this morning."

Suspect 2: Loretta Munch

Loretta Munch, a first-grade teacher, was born in Hurricane, Utah, near Zion National Park, the year the Japanese bombed Pearl Harbor.

"This theft is very disturbing," She told us. "I was planning to check out some of the new books to read to my grandson, Chuckie. He loves Virginia Lee Burton's books, especially *The Little House.* I buy all the books I can for him, but I can't afford very many on a teacher's salary."

Loretta Munch's alibi: "I was with my students all day. I stayed about an hour after school because I wanted to finish correcting my students' creative writing papers. Little Tommy Tinker had written a wonderful story about a green flamingo, who is an outcast because he's a different color than the other birds. It reminds me of *The Ugly Duckling*, which the Danish writer Hans Christian Andersen based on experiences in his own life."

Suspect 3: Paula Pucker

Paula Pucker, the president of the League of Literary Decency, was born in Broken Arrow, Oklahoma, a short distance southeast of Tulsa, the year that *The Bridge on the River Kwai* won the Academy Award for best motion picture.

"The League of Literary Decency is dedicated to protecting children from bad moral influences in literature," she explained. "I came to school to talk to the principal about our SMUT (Stop Morally Unfortunate Textbooks) campaign, but when I saw that Miss Shushingham was busy in the lobby, I took the opportunity to slip into the library for a look around."

"Well! I looked through the box of new books on the table, and I can't tell you how filthy and unsuitable they were. One book, *In the Night Kitchen* by Maurice Sendak, showed a young boy swimming stark naked in a gigantic milk bottle. I don't care if the author once won a Caldecott Medal; a man like that should be banned from writing children's books. And that horrible Samuel Clemens, that ruffian of a river boat pilot... Do you know he didn't even use his real name? What kind of men refuse to use their real names? Thieves and murderers!" She answered her own question. "Maybe even worse!"

Paula Pucker's alibi: "I have no alibi. I don't need an alibi. I am Mrs. Paula Pucker."

Suspect 4: Barry Bluejeans

Barry Bluejeans, the school's custodian, was born in Pittsfield, Massachusetts, not far from the Massachusetts-New York border, the year that *Why Mosquitoes Buzz in People's Ears: A West African Tale* won the Caldecott Medal.

"This is only a temporary job," he told us as he pushed a mop along the hallway floor. "When I save up enough money, I'm going to start my own business making and repairing violins. It's not like building a shelf, you know. The parts of a violin are glued together. There's not a nail or a screw used in the entire instrument. And you have to get the f-holes in the right place so the sound can escape from the belly of the instrument. Yes sir, someday I'm going to be as famous as the Italian, Antonio Stradivari. He made violins three hundred years ago, and more than 600 of them still exist."

"Not that it's easy to save money on the pitiful salary I get paid here," he complained. "If it weren't for my little business on the side, I'd never save a dime."

Barry's "little business on the side" is recycling. He goes through the school's trash looking for whatever can be sold: soda cans, pencils, paper, broken chairs and desks, and discarded textbooks, which he sells to a used-book dealer.

Barry Bluejean's alibi: "Sure, blame this theft on me. I was in the building after everyone else had left. I could have taken those books, but I didn't. Do you know why? They weren't there! I'm sure of that because I went into the library about 4:30 looking for an empty cardboard box to hold some stuff I'd found in the principal's wastebasket. There wasn't a cardboard box anywhere, not on the floor, not on the table, I thought there might be one in the library closet, but the closet door was locked."

The Solution

Poor Olive Shushingham finally went around the bend. She was so beside herself with worry that she didn't remember the correct Dewey Decimal numbers for the books in the school library, the name of the 1992 Newbery Medal winner, or even the year of her own birth. (Miss Shushingham is old, but she's not that old.) All those children pawing over the lovely library books with their "dirty little hands" drove her to the desperate act of locking the new books in the library closet, where they would be safe from damage.

Information about the suspects

Suspect 1—Olive Shushingham

Cape Girardeau, Missouri, is not on the Missouri River.

Agatha Christie was born in 1890.

The Dewey Decimal Classification System was developed by a librarian named Melvin, not Merwin, Dewey.

In the Dewey Decimal Classification System, art books would be found in the 700s, and science books would be in either the 500s or 600s.

Phyllis Reynolds Naylor won the Newbery Medal in 1992.

Suspect 2—Loretta Munch

Hurricane, Utah, is near Zion National Park.

The Japanese bombed Pearl Harbor in 1941.

Virginia Lee Burton wrote *The Little House*.

The Danish writer Hans Christian Andersen based The Ugly Duckling on experiences in his own life.

Suspect 3—Paula Pucker

Broken Arrow, Oklahoma, is a short distance southeast of Tulsa.

The *Bridge on the River Kwai* won the Academy Award for best motion picture in 1957.

Maurice Sendak won the Caldecott Medal for *Where the Wild Things Are*.

Samuel Langhorne Clemens was a Mississippi River pilot before he became a writer under the pseudonym of Mark Twain.

Suspect 4—Barry Bluejeans

Pittsfield, Massachusetts, is not far from the Massachusetts-New York border.

Why Mosquitoes Buzz in People's Ears: A West African Tale won the Caldecott Medal in 1976.

The parts of a violin are glued together. Nail and screws are not used.

The f-holes in the belly of the violin allow the sound to escape.

Antonio Stradivari, a native of Cremona, Italy, lived in the late 1600s, 300 years ago. More than 600 of the violins he made still exist today.

The Mystery of the Loosened Leash

The Crime

Booboo was Mikey Schnauzer's dog—a canine of decidedly mixed breeds. "I think she was part Chow Chow because her tongue was black," Mikey told us as he attempted to make a sketch of Booboo for a LOST DOG poster. "And, maybe she was part Irish wolfhound because she was so tall. And, she was pregnant. Mommy said I could keep all of her puppies. I hope whoever stole her takes good care of her until I get her back."

"Maybe no one stole her, Mikey," Mrs. Loretta Schnauser suggested quietly. "Maybe Booboo got tired of being tied to the porch, so she slipped off her leash and ran away."

"She wouldn't do that," Mikey answered firmly. "Somebody stole Booboo, and I'm going to find out who it was."

The Problem

Who took Booboo?

The Suspects

Suspect 1: Loretta Schnauzer

Loretta Schnauzer, Mikey's mother, was born in Prince Albert, which is south of Saskatoon, Saskatchewan, Canada, the year that Lucretia Coffin Mott died.

Mrs. Schnauzer runs a small but elegant antique business in her own home. "I specialize in Oriental rugs," she explained to us. "Especially Caucasian rugs, which are known for their soft, muted colors and bird motifs. I also sell Persian rugs, although they don't come from Persia anymore. As you probably know, Persia is now known as Jordan. I can give you a good price on those Oriental rugs in the corner. Booboo relieved herself on them, and I can't completely expunge the stains."

"Booboo followed Mikey home from school several months ago," Mrs. Schnauzer told us. "I didn't want a dog in the house, but Mikey had a tantrum until I conceded. I can't say no to Mikey. He's my only child."

Loretta Schauzer's alibi: "I drove to the airport with a crate of Oriental rugs I was shipping to an old friend in Cleveland."

Suspect 2: Felix Purrell

Felix Purrell, Mikey's neighbor on the left, was born in Cheektowaga, New York, near Lake Erie, the year *It's Like This, Cat* by Emily Cheney Neville won the Newbery Medal.

"So, Booboo's gone, is she? Good!" Felix Purrell said without a shred of sympathy for Mikey. "If I had my way, all the dogs on Maple Street would be rounded up and taken to the vet for euthanasia. I'm a cat person myself," he admitted, pointing to the felines that prowled around his yard. "I used to take care of the big cats at the San Diego Zoo. They're gorgeous creatures, and they're all different. The largest member of the cat family, the tiger, usually hunts at night and prefers to remain in the shadows. It seldom goes into open country like lions do. The leopards and the black leopards, which are called panthers, are good climbers and spend part of their time in trees. I wish I could keep a few as pets. They would have taken care of Booboo." He chuckled maliciously. "He wouldn't have barked at my precious kitties more than once."

Felix Purrell's alibi: "I took two of my darlings to the veterinarian for their yearly checkups."

Suspect 3: Margaret Rover

Margaret Rover, Mikey's neighbor on the right, was born in Prairie Village, Kansas, near the Kansas—Missouri border, the year George Orwell died.

"So Booboo ran away, did she? Good for her!" Mrs. Rover said without any sympathy for Mikey. "I hate to see dogs abused like that dog was. Mikey used to dress Booboo up like a clown and make her pull a wagon. And, he fed that poor thing Popsicles and potato chips. Imagine! That dog was carrying a litter of pups, and she was subsisting on junk food. It just wasn't right."

"I love dogs," Mrs. Rover admitted. "I love the big ones, like the St. Bernards, which were developed by monks in the Swiss Alps to help rescue lost travelers. They never wore casks of liquor around their necks, though," she said peevishly. "That's just a foolish story."

"And I love the little dogs," she said, bending down to pat her own Chihuahua on the head. "This is one of the smallest breeds of dog, though the smallest dog that ever lived was a miniature Yorkshire Terrier owned by a man in England. It was less than 4 inches long from the tip of its nose to the root of its tail. Imagine! You'd have to be careful not to step on a sweet thing like that, wouldn't you?"

Margaret Rover's alibi: "I drove out to the country to visit my sister that day. She has a large farm, where she breeds dogs."

Suspect 4: Harry Pith

Harry Pith, a salesman of biological supplies, was born in Mountain Home, Arkansas, near the Arkansas-Missouri border, the year Dr. Christiaan Neething Barnard performed the first successful human heart transplant.

"The specimens I sell to the local medical school are used to study comparative anatomy," Harry Pith told us. "Medical students need a wide range of animals for dissection: frogs, fetal pigs, cats, dogs, and cadavers. I do what I can to keep them supplied."

"It's not all that difficult to find frogs," Harry Pith admitted. "They live on every continent except Antarctica, though, of course, the tropical parts of the world are home to the greatest number of species. But sometimes it's hard to tell frogs and toads apart. In general, toads have broader, flatter bodies and darker, drier skin than frogs do. Frogs have smooth skin and toads are commonly covered with warts. Yech!" Pith shuddered. "I've been told you can't get warts by touching a toad, but I still insist on being paid extra for a load of toads."

Harry Pith's alibi: "I was at the pond on the end of Maple Street watching the frogs. There's a real nice population of amphibians there. Real nice."

The Solution

Loretta Schnauzer couldn't say no to her only son, especially when he threw himself on the floor and had a tantrum. But, neither could she tolerate the dog mess on the Oriental carpets she was trying to sell. In just a few weeks, Booboo was going to have a litter of puppies, and Mikey planned to keep all of them. Loretta could look forward to as many as twelve more little Booboos soiling her expensive merchandise unless she did something drastic.

Loretta crated something up and shipped it to an old friend in Cleveland. Chances are good that Booboo has a new home in Ohio.

Information about the suspects

Suspect 1—Loretta Schnauzer

Prince Albert is north, not south, of Saskatoon, Saskatchewan, Canada.

Lucretia Coffin Mott died in 1880.

Caucasian rugs are known for their bold geometric designs in bright colors, not for bird motifs in muted colors.

Persia is now known as Iran, not Jordan.

Suspect 2—Felix Purrell

Cheektowaga, New York, is near Lake Erie.

It's Like This, Cat by Emily Cheney Neville won the Newbery Medal in 1964.

The tiger, the largest member of the cat family, hunts at night and prefers to remain in the shadows.

Black leopards are called panthers. Leopards are good climbers and spend part of their time in trees.

Suspect 3—Margaret Rover

Prairie Village, Kansas, is near the Kansas–Missouri border.

George Orwell died in 1950.

St. Bernards were developed by monks in the Swiss Alps to help rescue lost travelers. They did not wear casks of liquor around their necks.

The Chihuahua is one of the smallest breeds of dog.

The smallest dog on record was a miniature Yorkshire Terrier owned by a man in England. It measured $3\,^3/4$" from the tip of its nose to the root of its tail and stood $2\,^1/2$" high at the shoulder.

Suspect 4—Harry Pith

Mountain Home, Arkansas is near the Arkansas-Missouri border.

Dr. Christiaan Neething Barnard performed the first successful human heart transplant in 1967.

Frogs live on every continent except Antarctica, but the tropical parts of the world are home to the greatest number of species.

It is sometimes hard to tell frogs and toads apart. In general, toads have broader, flatter bodies and darker, drier skin than frogs do. Frogs have smooth skin and toads are commonly covered with warts.

Touching a toad does not cause warts.

The Mystery of the Messed-Up Movie

The Crime

The Acme Insurance Company asked us to investigate a series of accidents that occurred during the filming of *Ramzilla*, a motion picture about a dinosaur that tramples through the jungles of Vietnam searching for prisoners of war. Several charges of dynamite went off incorrectly, leveling a village that had taken ten weeks to build; a faulty motor in the walking Ramzilla model caused the creature to fall over, crushing two jeeps and a motorcycle; improperly mixed fake quicksand swallowed two cameras and a cat; and a short-circuit in the electrical supply caused a fire that destroyed all of the costumes.

Even more disturbing, however, was a series of injuries sustained by the actors: Eva Cleava, the leading lady, broke her ankle and cut her lip when she tripped over a misplaced machine gun; Danny Drago, the leading man, had an allergic reaction to his makeup, which contained pureed poison ivy; and the entire cast got food poisoning from tuna fish sandwiches when the refrigerator in the food cart was disconnected.

Fearing that an accident would eventually prove fatal, the studio canceled its contract with the producer. The film, however, had been insured. Ned Narcisso turned in the following list of expenses to the insurance company:

Eva Cleava's salary–$200,000

Danny Drago's salary–$500,000

Two cameras–$185,000

Two jeeps–$40,000

Costumes–$116,000

Damaged Ramzilla model–$1,365,000

The Problem

Who caused the accidents on the set of *Ramzilla?*

The Suspects

Suspect 1: Ned Narcisso

Ned Narcisso, the producer of the movie, was born in Reno, which is south of Carson City, Nevada, the year Cecil Blount DeMille was born.

He was once an electrical engineer, but he gave up his job with General Electric to pursue a career in Hollywood. He has had six wives and is presently married to Melba Peach, a cosmetician he met during the filming of his previous movie, The Venus's-Flytrap that Ate Peoria.

"*The Venus's-Flytrap that Ate Peoria* was treated badly by the critics," Ned complained. "We did a fabulous job, especially with the special effects. I sent my crew to Africa to photograph the Venus's-Flytrap in its natural environment. Then we superimposed that film over shots of Peoria. We chose Peoria because my camera people liked the way the sunlight reflected off the nearby Sierra Madre mountains. But do you think the critics appreciated any of that artistry? They're Philstines, every one of them! The film lost money, and after that the studio executives stopped answering my phone calls."

"But, I've got five ex-wives demanding alimony. I can't afford to stop making movies. I pawned everything I owned to finance *Ramzilla.*"

Ned Narcisso's alibi: "I was on the set when all the accidents occurred. I'm the producer. I'm supposed to be here! But, I'm the last person on earth who'd sabotage this movie. This was to be my comeback. I expected to make a fortune at the box office, and I wouldn't have been surprised by an Academy Award nomination for best motion picture of the year."

Suspect 2: Eva Cleava

Eva Cleava, the leading lady, was born Hildegard May Smith, in Sainte Genevieve, Missouri, near the Mississippi River. Although she was born the year that *All About Eve* won the Academy Award for best motion picture, Eva had been playing the role of ingenues for the past 25 years.

Eva took the role of a munitions expert who runs an orphanage in *Ramzilla* because she felt the part would display her depth and versatility as an actress. "I wanted to change my screen image from the Mary Pickford 'America's sweetheart' type to the mysterious, tragic Greta Garbo type," Eva Cleava explained. "Unfortunately, the script for *Ramzilla* didn't give me very much to work with. I had a total of twenty lines, and at least six of them were repeats of 'Oh! Oh! The beast is coming!' Oh well," she shrugged philosophically. "Ned was paying me $20,000, and I haven't been offered any other movie roles in the past three years."

Eva Cleava's alibi: "Darling! you can't suspect me of doing all those horrible things to the movie! I was the star! Besides, I would never have done anything to injure my face. If I had been responsible for the sabotage, I would have made sure Danny Drago tripped over the machine gun. His face could use a little rearranging."

Suspect 3: Danny Drago

Danny Drago, the leading man, was born Danny Dragoviski in Mar del Plata, Argentina, on the shores of the Atlantic Ocean, the year Duke Ellington died.

Danny Drago signed a contract to play the male lead in *Ramzilla* before he rocketed to success in the lead role in *Surfer Nerds*. He has made no secret of his feelings. He hated the film, hated the producer, and, most especially, he hated Eva Cleava. He admitted that he told his co-star, "You and me, we're both turkeys, Eva. The difference is, I'm a wild turkey who can fly. You're a fat, stupid domesticated turkey who can't get off the ground."

"Like, I've got a reputation to uphold, you know," he mumbled. "I went to a past-lives therapist, and she told me I was James Dean born all over again in a new body. He was, like, you know, brooding and intense and rebellious. He starred in three films, and then he got himself kinda' killed in a car accident, and his soul went into limbo waitin' around for nineteen years until I came along. So, I'm destined for greatness, and I don't have time for this *Ramzilla* garbage."

Danny Drago's alibi: "I wish I had sabotaged the movie, but I didn't do it, man. Like, I'm an actor, see, not a terrorist. But, if you want to know who had a reason, go talk to Eva the Ego. She was a down-and-out actress who couldn't get herself interviewed if she jumped off a bridge, but now she's playing the role of martyr for all the reporters who have come around."

Suspect 4: Harry Henson

Harry Henson, the prop man, was born in Iron Mountain, Michigan, near the Wisconsin border, the year Al Capone died.

He has worked on six of Ned Narcisso's movies, including *The Venus's-Flytrap that Ate Peoria*. During the six weeks it took to make that film, his wife Melba Peach divorced him to marry Ned Narcisso. Harry isn't bitter. He claims that Ned did him a favor.

"My marriage was a mistake," Ned admitted with a shrug. "Melba is a sweet kid, but her father was driving me nuts. He's an agriculturist here in California, which is the top U.S. state in terms of peach production, and he kept sending us crates and crates of fruit. I was getting pretty sick of eating the matured ovaries of flowers. When Melba told me she wanted a divorce, I told her, 'No hard feelings, Mel. I figured that men and peaches come in two varieties—clingstone and freestone. And I'm cut out to be a freestone.' After she left, I went out for a pepperoni pizza."

Harry Henson's alibi: "I was on the set when all the accidents happened, but I didn't have to sabotage the picture. It would have bombed anyway, and I'll tell you why. Everything was cheap. Ned got the cameras for $50 each at a going-out-of-business sale. He picked the jeeps up in the Beverly Hills junkyard. The costumes were borrowed from a local high school's drama club. The Ramzilla model was made out of cardboard and aluminum foil. The entire village cost maybe $200 to put up. The guns were the kind of plastic toys you can buy at Toys-R-Us. All the props were so cheap and sleazy the film would have been laughed at if it had ever been shown in theaters."

The Solution

Ned Narcisso intended to make money from *Ramzilla*, but not from box office receipts. He paid as little as possible for actors, equipment, and props, intending to have the insurance company reimburse him much more than his actual costs when the film was canceled. Because he was an electrical engineer before he became a director, he knew how to sabotage the motors and wiring. His wife may have helped him whip up the batch of poison ivy makeup for Danny Drago.

Information about the suspects

Suspect 1—Ned Narcisso

Reno, Nevada, is north, not south, of Carson City.

Cecil Blount DeMille was born in 1881.

Venus's-Flytrap is not an African plant. It grows in a small coastal area of North and South Carolina.

The Sierra Madre mountains are located in Mexico, a long way from Peoria, Arizona, and even farther from Peoria, Illinois.

Suspect 2—Eva Cleava

Sainte Genevieve, Missouri, is near the Mississippi River.

All About Eve won the Academy Award for best motion picture in 1950.

Mary Pickford was known as "America's sweetheart."

Greta Garbo became famous for playing mysterious women who meet tragic ends.

Suspect 3—Danny Drago

Mar del Plata, Argentina, is on the shores of the Atlantic Ocean.

Duke Ellington died in 1974.

Wild turkeys can fly. Domesticated turkeys usually cannot.

James Dean portrayed young men who were brooding, intense, and rebellious.

James Dean starred in three films before he was killed in a car accident.

James Dean died in 1955. Danny Drago was born in 1974. Nineteen years passed between those two dates.

Suspect 4—Harry Henson

Iron Mountain, Michigan, is near the Wisconsin border.

Al Capone died in 1947.

California is the top U.S. state in terms of peach production.

Fruit is the matured ovary of a flower.

There are two varieties of peaches—clingstone and freestone.

The Mystery of the Mined Mall

The Crime

The Shoplex Development Company's new shopping mall was plagued by problems right from the start. Granite outcroppings on the site required blasting with large amounts of dynamite. A nearby swamp produced a breed of mega-mosquitoes that drove the construction workers crazy. The union went on strike, demanding safer working conditions. Supplies, including lumber, windows, and dynamite, were stolen from the construction site. The architect was so infuriated by changes made in his design that he showed up at the site and screamed at the construction workers.

Native American activists picketed the shopping mall because they believed it was being built on the site of one of their burial grounds.

But, despite all of the problems and construction delays, the shopping mall was finished on March 27. On March 30, it exploded.

The Problem

Who blew up the mall?

The Suspects

Suspect 1: Howard Rook

Howard Rook, the architect who designed the shopping mall, was born in Cavalier, North Dakota, which is in the southwest corner of the state, the year John Lennon died.

He was not pleased with the changes the developer had made in his designs. "My design was elegant and graceful, much like the buildings that were designed by my former teacher Inigo Jones," he complained to us. "But, the Shoplex Development Company decided to make a few changes to save money. Here a change, there a change… Before I knew what was happening, they had turned my lovely building into an ugly slab of brick and glass. I was ashamed to have my name connected with the sprawling mess."

"There was a similar incident in Frank Lloyd Wright's autobiography, *The Architect*," he continued. "Wright was unhappy with the changes that were made to his design for the Imperial Hotel in Tokyo. Fortunately, the building crumbled during the 1923 earthquake in Japan."

Howard Rook's alibi: "I was at home that night reading *Architectural Digest* magazine."

Suspect 2: Feather Grey Fox

Feather Grey Fox, the Native American activist who led the fight to prevent the building of the shopping mall, was born in San Juan Capistrano, California, on the coast of the Pacific Ocean, the year *Midnight Cowboy* won the Academy Award for best motion picture.

"Some Native American tribes feared ghosts of the dead," Feather Grey Fox told us. "But, most Native Americans did not give much thought to life after death or the idea of heaven. 'The happy hunting ground' was the invention of white settlers. Still, my ancestors from the Diegueno tribe are buried on that land, and it is obscene to think of them resting beneath an Orange Julius stand or a Kaybee Toy Store."

Feather Grey Fox's alibi: "I was camping in the mountains, communing with the spirits."

Suspect 3: Gregory Grinchley

Gregory Grinchley, the developer who built the mall, was born in Oshkosh, Wisconsin, near Lake Winnebago, the year Charles S. Woolworth died.

"I'll tell you what's wrong with Howard Rook," Gregory Grinchley told us. "He thinks an architect is God and the building blueprints are the Decalogue handed down to Moses on Mt. Sinai. But I figure, if I'm paying, I'm saying, know what I mean? I told him I wanted the kind of building Buckminster Fuller used to design—one of those big geodesic dome kind of things with plenty of space for merchandise. Instead, Rook gave me a design for something that looks like an Italian palace with an enormous indoor garden. This is a shopping center, for crying out loud, not an indoor arboretum."

"The Indian Rock Shopping Center has been a nightmare of a project ever since we started," Gregory Grinchley complained. First, we had those Indian fruitcakes picketing the site. Then, Rook started screaming about the changes we made in his designs. So, we took out the skylights and the fountains and the waterfalls and the gardens. So what? We put in a McDonald's restaurant. Doesn't that count for something?"

"After all that trouble, no one wanted to rent store space in the building. At least the insurance company paid off after the explosion. I'm going to take the money and build a shopping mall some place where people appreciate the important things in life."

Gregory Grinhchley's alibi: "I was at home watching 'Bowling for Bucks' on television."

Suspect 4: Bartholomew Barth

Bartholomew Barth, a former employee of the Shoplex Development Company, was born in Eagle Pass, Texas, on the banks of the Rio Grande, the year an explosion on a pier in Texas City, Texas, killed 561 people.

"I don't have anything good to say about the Shoplex Development Company," he admitted. "I was active in the Construction Workers Union and helped organize a strike for better working conditions. They had us using straight dynamite," he explained. "We were demanding a switch to ammonia dynamite because it is safer than straight dynamite and produces fewer toxic fumes. Grinchley gave in and authorized the switch, and then a few days later he had me fired for leading the job walk-out."

"Oh, he says different," Bartholomew Barth said cynically. "He says I was fired because I drank on the job, but who wouldn't drink? All those spooky stories about the land being a Native American burial ground gave me the willies. I've got a much better job now with a company that's putting in a new shopping mall a few miles down the road."

Bartholomew Barth's alibi: "I was at home watching the John Wayne movie *True Grit* on television." It's the performance for which he won an Academy Award."

The Solution

Howard Rook couldn't stand what the Shoplex Development Company had done to his design for the shopping mall. The company had taken out the waterfalls, the skylights, the gardens, and the fountains. What could have been a beautiful building ended up looking more like a concrete bunker. On the night of March 30, Howard Rook decided to destroy Shoplex's building as completely as Shoplex had destroyed his architectural plans. He knew the building well enough to know where to put the dynamite to do the most damage.

Information about the suspects

Suspect 1—Howard Rook

Cavalier, North Dakota, is in the northeast, not the southwest, corner of the state.

John Lennon died in 1980.

Inigo Jones died in 1652, long before Howard Rook was born.

Frank Lloyd Wright's autobiography was titled *Autobiography.*

There is no evidence that Frank Lloyd Wright was displeased with the final building of the Imperial Hotel.

The Imperial Hotel was one of the few buildings in Tokyo that survived the 1923 earthquake undamaged.

Suspect 2—Feather Grey Fox

San Juan Capistrano, California, is on the coast of the Pacific Ocean.

Midnight Cowboy won the Academy Award for best motion picture in 1969.

According to *The World Book Encyclopedia,* some Native American tribes feared ghosts of the dead, but most Native Americans did not give much thought to life after death or the idea of heaven. "The happy hunting ground" was the invention of white settlers.

The Diegueno Indians lived in southern California and northern Mexico.

Suspect 3—Gregory Grinchley

Oshkosh, Wisconsin, is near Lake Winnebago.

Charles S. Woolworth died in 1947.

The Decalogue, more commonly known as the Ten Commandments, was handed down to Moses on Mt. Sinai.

Buckminster Fuller designed the geodesic dome.

Suspect 4—Bartholomew Barth

Eagle Pass, Texas, is on the banks of Rio Grande.

In 1947, an explosion on a pier in Texas City, Texas, killed 561 people.

Ammonia dynamite is safer than straight dynamite and produces fewer toxic fumes.

John Wayne won an Academy Award for his performance in *True Grit.*

The Mystery of the Pooped Pyrotechnics

The Crime

This year's Fourth of July fireworks display at the fairgrounds was billed as "the *BIGGEST* and *BRIGHTEST* ever!" At exactly 10:30 P.M., Jim Crack signaled his crew to light the fuses. The first rocket whistled upward, leaving a trail of smoke behind it. Then, as the crowd held its breath in anticipation, it slowed, arced downward, and hit the ground with a dull thud. One skyrocket after another was lit, but none of them produced the booms and flares and sizzles that the crowd expected. Most of the skyrockets never got out of their launching tubes.

"They were sabotaged," Jim Crack told us later, after he had examined some of the failed rockets. "The finely textured gunpowder that is supposed to explode the rockets in the air had been removed. We found it heaped up in Willard Tremor's backyard. The town was supposed to pay me $100,000 for these pyrotechnics. If they refuse to pay, my company will be bankrupt."

The Problem

Who ruined the fireworks?

The Suspects

Suspect 1: Fargo Very

Fargo Very, the president of a rival fireworks company, was born in Waterloo, Iowa, west of Dubuque, the year that Tennesse Williams won the Pulitzer Prize for *Cat on a Hot Tin Roof.*

"It serves the town right," Fargo grumbled. "My family has been doing the town's annual fireworks display ever since Congress declared Independence Day a legal federal holiday in 1941. A good show at a good price—that's always been our motto. This year is the town's centennial, and the townspeople wanted something extra fancy. But, they didn't want to pay more than they paid for last year's display. I told them I couldn't give them what they wanted at that price.

"The Jim Crack Company came along and promised them what they wanted. I warned them that Jim Crack's price was too low to be realistic, but you know how politicians are—they can't resist a bargain. The Mayor even had the gall to ask me to play my flugelhorn at the beginning of the fireworks display. Only, he didn't say, 'flugelhorn.' He said, 'Could you play that cornet of yours?' Any fool knows that, while the flugelhorn may look something like a cornet, it's actually a member of the bugle family."

Fargo Very's alibi: "I drove my camper out to the fairgrounds on Independence Day. I was curious about Jim Crack's rockets, so I wandered down into the ravine where the launching equipment was being set up and introduced myself to his work crew. They were barely more than kids and badly underpaid for the kind of dangerous work they were doing. That's how Jim Crack keeps his expenses down. My argument was with Jim Crack, not with his crew, so I invited them all back to my camper for a few beers."

Suspect 2: Bertha Fusee

Bertha Fusee, the sheriff, was born in Madawaska, on the northern border of Maine, the year President John F. Kennedy was assassinated.

"I don't like fireworks," Bertha Fusee told us. "And, this year's display was going to be worse than ever. 'Bigger! Brighter! Better!'" she said, pointing to a battered sign on a nearby telephone pole. "The Chamber of Commerce might as well have written, 'More dangerous! More deadly! More chance of injury and fire!'"

"There was a horrible explosion in a fireworks factory in Hallett, Oklahoma, in 1985," she told us. "Twenty-one people died. I was living there with my husband, who was a munitions expert for a mining company, when it happened. No one who saw that tragedy could ever again think of fireworks as harmless, frivolous fun."

Bertha Fusee's alibi: "I was on duty at the fairground that day. I visited the animal exhibits to see if they had any karakul sheep. Karakul lambs are often killed when they are less than ten days old because that's when their fur is the most valuable. I wanted to make it perfectly clear that there would be no lamb killing in my town. When I came out, I saw that a large crowd had gathered, so I went down into the ravine to check on the company's security procedures. I found children climbing all over the Jim Crack Company's equipment. There wasn't a Jim Crack employee in sight! I chased the kids away and checked for damage. Then, I went to find Mr. Crack to apprise him of our town ordinance on unsecured explosives."

Suspect 3: Willard Tremor

Willard Tremor, a demolition expert during the Vietnam War, was born in Bossier City, Louisiana, near the Red River, the year World War II ended. He lives in a trailer next to the fairgrounds.

"I've got a nervous twitch," Willard apologized. "It's particularly bad in July. Every time a kid sets off a firecracker, I think I'm back in Hue, Vietnam, in 1968, during the Tet Offensive. I dive for cover and pray I can still see daylight when the shooting is over."

Willard Tremor's alibi: "When I saw the Jim Crack Company setting up its equipment in the ravine between the fairgrounds and my backyard, I knew I was going to have a hard night. I got my backpack and my sleeping bag and took off for the hills. I collected some pine cones while I was there," he told us, showing us a sack of cones that were about four inches long. "These are female pine cones. Male pine cones are much smaller."

Suspect 4: Clarence Sizzle

Clarence Sizzle, the former foreman for the Jim Crack Company, was born in Winooski, Vermont, east of Montpelier, the year Alfred Bernhard Nobel died.

"I'm glad that's all that went wrong." Clarence Sizzle seemed relieved about the inoperable skyrockets. "I had a premonition about that job. Jim Crack was cutting too many corners. Right from the beginning, he skimped on the strontium in the yellow skyrockets and the charcoal compounds in the blue ones. Then, he hired too few men, and those men were too inexperienced to handle explosives properly. When he decided to set up the launching equipment in the ravine, I had to speak my mind. I told him it was too secluded. A kid could wander down there without being seen and accidentally get blown to pieces."

Clarence Sizzle's alibi: "I spent the morning trying to talk some sense into Jim Crack. Then he fired me, and I got in my car and drove away. 'Good riddance,' I told myself. But, I knew I'd feel bad if something happened and I hadn't tried to stop it. So, after a few hours of driving, I turned the car around and went back. I got there just in time to hear *The Battle Hymn of the Republic*, the words of which were written by Katharine Lee Bates, being played rather badly on some kind of bugle."

The Solution

Clarence Sizzle had a premonition about that night's fireworks display. Jim Crack had cut too many corners in the construction of the skyrockets. He had hired too few men, and the ones he had hired were inexperienced. Even the location of the launching equipment in the ravine worried him; it was too secluded. Curious children could slip into the ravine unnoticed and accidentally set off one of the rockets.

Clarence did his best to convince Jim Crack to see the problems, but Jim Crack fired him instead. Clarence drove away angry, but he didn't get far before his conscience began to bother him. He turned the car around and returned to the fairgrounds. Slipping unnoticed into the ravine (the work crew was drinking beer in Fargo Very's Camper, the children had been chased away by the sheriff, and Bertha Fusee had gone in search of Jim Crack), Clarence emptied the gunpowder out of the fireworks to make them as harmless as possible.

He dumped the gunpowder in Willard Tremor's backyard because he didn't know what else to do with it. Maybe he had heard that Willard Tremor was a demolition expert in the army and thought he would know enough not to blow himself up with it when he found it there.

Information about the suspects

Suspect 1—Fargo Very
Waterloo, Iowa, is west of Dubuque.

Tennessee Williams won a Pulitzer Prize in Drama for *Cat on a Hot Tin Roof* in 1955.

Congress declared Independence Day a legal federal holiday in 1941.

Although the flugelhorn looks something like a cornet, it's actually a member of the bugle family.

Suspect 2—Bertha Fusee
Madawaska is on the northern border of Maine.

President John F. Kennedy was assassinated in 1963.

Twenty-one people died when a fireworks factory exploded in Hallett, Oklahoma, in 1985.

Karakul lambs are often killed when they are under ten days old, when their fur is the most valuable for making Persian lamb coats.

Suspect 3—Willard Tremor
Bossier City, Louisiana, is near the Red River.

World War II ended in 1945.

Fighting was heavy in Hue, Vietnam, during the Tet Offensive of 1968.

Female pine cones are the large scaly cones most people think of as pine cones, Male cones are usually smaller than one inch and produce pollen in the spring.

Suspect 4—Clarence Sizzle
Winooski, Vermont, is west, not east, of Montpelier.

Alfred Bernhard Nobel died in 1896.

Strontium is used in red skyrockets, not yellow ones.

Katharine Lee Bates wrote the words to *America, the Beautiful.* The words to *The Battle Hymn of the Republic* were written by Julia Ward Howe.

The Mystery of the Gooey Glove

The Crime

Tyrone Rexall was the best player on the Diamonds baseball team. He could hit. He could catch. He could field. He could run. In fact, he was so formidable that he had been dubbed "Tyronosaurus Rex" by the sports reporters from the local papers. Everyone predicted that Tyrone would trample his opponents in the upcoming championship game.

Imagine everyone's surprise when he tripped and fell flat on his face while running to first base. Later in the game, he scooped up the baseball in the outfield, only to have it stick fast to his glove. All through the game, he fidgeted as he tried desperately to follow the owner's most important rule: Don't ever scratch in public.

After the game, which the Diamonds lost by an embarrassingly large margin, Tyrone called a press conference to accuse "an unknown saboteur" of being responsible for his disgraceful performance on the field. He claimed that the seams of his shoes had been weakened so they'd fall apart with the most minimal activity, his glove had been coated with a sticky glue, and itching powder had been put in his uniform. "Someone made me lose that championship," Tyrone Rexall muttered. "And when I find out who it was, I'm going to throw him clear across the infield."

The Problem

Who is to blame for Tyrone's poor performance?

The Suspects

Suspect 1: Rusty Rassmussen

Rusty Rassmussen, an ex-player for the Diamonds, was born in Waukegan, Illinois, which is located on the banks of the Ohio River, the year Satchel Paige was born.

"I don't have any great regard for Tyrone Rexall," Rusty Rassmussen spit out the name of his former colleague as if he found it odious. "That pompous, posturing nincompoop had me kicked off the team, all because we had a disagreement about a game of poker."

"I was holding three aces and two kings. Tyrone had the three, four, five, six, and seven of spades, and he claims he won the hand. Any jerk knows a full house beats a straight flush, but Tyrone pitched a fit about it. He called me a charlatan and slandered me in front of the other guys. Then, he told Mrs. Lord, the owner of the Diamonds team, that he couldn't play on a team with someone he couldn't trust, so either I had to be fired, or he would quit. Well, my batting average wasn't real high, but Tyrone had a shot at breaking the .406 batting average Ted Williams set back in 1951, so I guess Mrs. Lord figured I was expendable."

Rusty Rassmussen's alibi: "I had tickets for the game, and since I was there early, I decided to stop by the locker room and see some of the guys. I left before Tyrone showed up because I still hold a grudge about the way he treated me. I've got such a bad temper that there's no telling what I would have done if I had seen Tyrone face to face."

Suspect 2: Mimi Dew

Mimi Dew, a kindergarten teacher, was born in Yazoo City, Mississippi, south of Clarksdale, the year Earle Stanley Gardner died.

"I loved Tyrone when he was a nobody." Mimi Dew used a lacy handkerchief to wipe away a tear. "He used to come to my house after a hard, discouraging day and threaten to quit baseball. When he did that, I would serve him a big plate of chocolate chip cookies and recite all his favorite poems from childhood. He liked "Little Orphant Annie" by James Whitcomb Riley and "Wynken, Blynken, and Nod" by Eugene Field the best."

"But, when he got famous, he didn't have time for me anymore. He was too busy going to fancy parties and eating caviar to remember the simple, happy times we used to have together. I'd do anything to have my Tyrone back the way he used to be." Mimi succumbed to sobs. "Anything!"

Mimi Dew's alibi: "I went to the Diamonds' locker room before the championship to beg Tyrone to come back to me. But, then I realized how pathetic I was being. A woman can't beg a man to love her. I left before he arrived."

Suspect 3: Martha Lord

Martha Lord, owner of the Diamonds baseball team, was born in Chula Vista, California, near the Mexican border, the year Carolyn S. Bailey won the Newbery medal for Miss Hickory.

"Come in and sit down. I don't have all day," Mrs. Lord said tersely. "The first thing you should know about Tyrone Rexall is that he has the potential to be a great baseball player. He could be another Babe Ruth, who had a .342 lifetime batting average. He could be another Hank Aaron, who led the National League in home runs in 1957, 1963, 1966, 1967."

"He could be anything he put his mind to," Mrs. Lord continued. "But, Tyrone is also an enfant terrible. He was coming into my office every day with new demands. 'Fire him, hire him. I want this, I insist on that.' He was becoming a first-class pain in the buttocks. I was amused to see him taken down a peg. However, we lost the championship, and that does not amuse me."

Martha Lord's alibi: "I was in my office going over budget figures. Tyrone's demands had become increasingly expensive, and I was wondering what to do about them."

Suspect 4: Kent Clarkson

Kent Clarkson, the sports reporter for the local paper, was born in Council Bluffs, Iowa, on the banks of the Missouri River, the year that Edward R. Murrow died.

"I love baseball," Kent Clarkson told us vehemently. "I especially love the heroic people who have made the game what it is today: Jack Roosevelt Robinson, who was the first African-American to play the major leagues, and Roberto Clemente, who died in a plane crash on his way to aid earthquake victims. I thought Tyrone Rexall was going to be another man like them—a man whose life story would be worth writing about."

"But, success ruined Tyrone." Kent Clarkson shook his head disapprovingly. "Do you know that Tyrone has been charging kids $15 for his autograph? Not that it's worth a nickel right now," he chuckled with malicious satisfaction. "In this profession, you're no better than your last game. Tyronosaurus Rex is finding that out the hard way."

Kent Clarkson's alibi: "I went to the Diamonds' locker room before the game to ask Tyrone if I could interview him for a book about his life. Tyrone said sure, but he wanted 75 percent of my royalties. He said that since it was his life, he should be the one to get the profits. I was so disgusted I went over to the other team's locker room to interview its pitcher."

The Solution

By his own admission, Rusty Rassmussen had a temper and still bore a grudge against Tyrone Rexall. Tyrone had had him fired after their dispute about the poker hand, and Rusty was out for revenge. What better revenge could there be than to let Tyronosaurus Rex make a fool of himself during the best attended game of the season?

Rusty went to the locker room, ostensibly to see his friends. But, while they were showering and getting dressed, he set to work sabotaging Tyrone Rexall's gear. Then, he took a seat in the stands to enjoy Tyrone's humiliation.

Information about the suspects

Suspect 1—Rusty Rassmussen

Waukegan, Illinois, is located near Lake Michigan, not on the banks of the Ohio River.

The exact date of Satchel Paige's birth is in question, but he was born sometime around 1906.

Rusty was wrong about a full house beating a straight flush. Tyrone's straight flush (five cards in sequence, all of the same suit) beat Rusty's full house (three aces and two kings).

Ted Williams set a record with a .406 batting average, but it was in 1941, not 1951.

Suspect 2—Mimi Dew

Yazoo City, Mississippi, is south of Clarksdale.

Earle Stanley Gardner died in 1970.

James Whitcomb Riley wrote "Little Orphant Annie."

Eugene Field wrote "Wynken, Blynken, and Nod."

Suspect 3—Martha Lord

Chula Vista, California, is near the Mexican border.

Carolyn S. Bailey won the Newbery Medal for *Miss Hickory* in 1947.

Babe Ruth had a .342 lifetime batting average.

Hank Aaron led the National League in home runs in 1957, 1963, 1966, and 1967.

Suspect 4—Kent Clarkson

Council Bluffs, Iowa, is on the banks of the Missouri River.

Edward R. Murrow died in 1965.

Jackie Robinson was the first African-American to play in the major leagues.

Roberto Clemente died in a plane crash on his way to aid earthquake victims in Nicaragua.

Intermediate

Mysteries

The Mystery of the Submerging Sea Serpent

The Crime

The seaside community of Nessville, where the Ness brothers were born and raised, had been a thriving tourist town during the 1960s and 1970s. But, a number of events had driven the tourist trade away: toxic wastes had washed up on the beaches; high levels of carcinogens had been found in the local sport fish; and a new superhighway bypassed the small town, diverting tourists to the brightly lit casinos of Atlantic City.

It looked as if tourism in Nessville was as extinct as a dinosaur until a sea serpent surfaced within view of the porch of the Sea Breeze Hotel one foggy evening in June. Within a week, the town was bustling with reporters and tourists, all eager to view the sea serpent, who obligingly appeared every day at dusk.

Then, as quickly as it had come, the serpent disappeared forever. Townspeople claimed that it had been chased away by the noisy and intrusive marine biologists who had come to capture it. The marine biologists said they had taken sonar readings of what looked like railroad tracks along the bottom of the harbor. In their opinion, the Nessville Serpent had never been anything but a hoax.

The Problem

Who created the Nessville Serpent hoax?

The Suspects

Suspect 1: Brandon Ness

Brandon Ness, the owner of the Sea Breeze Hotel, was born in Nessville, New Jersey. Nessville is so small that it is not listed in any atlas, but it is located somewhere between Atlantic City and Cape May, New Jersey. Brandon was born the year that W. C. Fields died.

"My brothers and I were dining together on the porch of my hotel that fateful evening in June," Brandon explained. "The fog lifted for just a moment, and that's when we saw it—a sea serpent the size of a school bus. I used to be interested in dinosaurs when I was a kid, so I was immediately struck by the resemblance of the Nessville Serpent to the apatosaurus, which lived during the Cenozoic Era."

Brandon Ness' alibi: "I was right here on the porch of my hotel every night the Nessville Serpent was sighted. I told my guests where to look and what to expect when he appeared."

Suspect 2: Beecham Ness

Beecham Ness, the editor of the *Nessville Gazette*, was born in Nessville, New Jersey. The town is located at the same longitude as Hackensack, New Jersey. Beecham was born the year that D. W. Griffith died.

"Yes sir, it's been quite a time," Beecham Ness admitted with a grin. "One minute we're living in a quiet, half-forgotten town, and the next minute we've got reporters and tourists all over the place. Rooms in Brandon's hotel have been full all summer. The *Nessville Gazette* has been selling like hotcakes. Billy's Toy and Gadget Shop has been doing a land-office business, especially with his motorized replicas of the Nessville Serpent. All this excitement has been real good for everyone in town."

Beecham Ness' alibi: "I was right there on the porch when all of us first saw it. I wrote the first news stories about the Nessville Serpent's appearance. Then, when the reporters from the big city papers started showing up, I gave them all the help I could. I told them all about the coelacanths we used to pull out of these waters when we were kids."

Suspect 3: Beauregard Ness

Beauregard Ness, the sheriff of Nessville, was born in Nessville, New Jersey, which is located at the same latitude as Atlantic City, New Jersey. Beauregard was born the year that Al Jolson died.

"I was on the porch with my brothers when we saw a huge creature surface over by Bleeker Rock. It swam in toward shore until it reached the channel buoys. Then it submerged."

"It was a real pretty sight," Beauregard Ness said laconically. "And, it was real good for the town. Then, the marine biologists started pouring in from the big cities. I didn't say anything when they ran their boats back and forth across the harbor to take sonar readings, even though I didn't approve. I don't think anyone really knows what effect those infrared light rays have on fish."

"I was perturbed when the biologists started doubting the veracity of people in this town, but I didn't bother them until they tried to get into Brandon's boat house. If Brandon wanted to keep it padlocked, then he had a right to keep it padlocked.

This is America, and a property owner's got a right to privacy."

Beauregard Ness' alibi: "I saw the Nessville Serpent from time to time, but I didn't have a lot of time to spend on the porch of Brandon's hotel. In addition to being sheriff here in Nessville, I'm also a security guard for the railroad. Near the end of the summer, I was kept even busier than usual following those marine biologists around to keep them from interfering with the rights of local residents."

Suspect 4: Billy Ness

Billy Ness, the owner of Billy's Toy and Gadget Shop, was born in Nessville, New Jersey. The town is very small, but it is located about 55 miles south of Asbury Park, New Jersey. Billy was born the year that *The Greatest Show on Earth* won the Academy Award for the best motion picture.

"We used to have such a wonderful time here in Nessville," Billy told us wistfully. "My brothers and I would snorkel and scuba dive in the harbor. Sometimes we'd catch a lungfish for our supper."

"And, every summer we'd build a mechanized float for the Nessville Fourth of July parade. Brandon would come up with the idea. Beauregard used to scrounge around for the materials. I'd design the pulleys and motors. Beecham would paint the signs. Brandon and Beecham would drive the truck while Beauregard and I hid underneath the float and worked the switches. We won a prize just about every year. It was a wonderful childhood. I wish Nessville could have kept on being the terrific town it used to be."

Billy Ness' alibi: "I saw the Nessville Serpent that first time, but after the tourists and reporter started coming to town, I didn't go back to watch it from the porch of Brandon's hotel. I guess I'm kind of shy. Anyhow, I was busy making mechanical gadgets for the tourist. They really liked the replica of the Nessville Serpent. I sold so many of them that I hired 30 people from the town to help me turn them out."

The Solution

Brandon, Beecham, Beauregard, and Billy were close and devoted brothers. As children they formed an unbeatable team for the annual Fourth of July float competition: Brandon came up with the ideas, Billy designed the float, Beauregard scrounged the materials, and Beecham painted the signs. Their roles in the Nessville Serpent hoax were much the same.

Brandon got the idea for the sea serpent as he gazed out over the fog-shrouded Nessville Harbor. Billy thought he could build a mechanized serpent if he could get the materials he needed. Beauregard, as security guard for the railroad, knew where to get materials, including rails for an underwater track. Beecham wrote the newspaper articles that would later attract reporters and tourists to the town.

They were all adept at scuba diving, and they may have had help from other townspeople when they laid the underwater tracks. Their scheme, which was intended to revive the tourist industry in a dying town, was meant to help everyone in Nessville, not just the four Ness brothers.

Once the mechanized sea serpent had been built and the tourists started streaming into town, the four brothers settled into a daily routine. Brandon stood on the porch with his guests telling them where to look and what to expect when the Nessville Serpent surfaced in the waning light of dusk. (No doubt many of them saw exactly what they were told they'd see.) Brandon was helpful to the reporters, giving them "facts" for their stories. Billy, who was never on the porch during the tourists' sightings of the serpent, was busy pulling the switches that made the serpent run along the underwater track. Beaurgard, in his official role as the sheriff of Nessville, kept a close watch over the suspicious marine biologists, making sure they didn't unlock and enter Brandon's boat house, where the mechanized serpent was kept.

It's too bad the brothers weren't as knowledgeable about geography as they were about the mechanical contraptions. A town 55 miles south of Asbury park, New Jersey, that was on the same longitude as Hackensack and the same latitude as Atlantic City, would not lie between Atlantic City and Cape May. It would be located under the waters of the Atlantic Ocean.

Information about the suspects

Suspect 1—Brandon Ness
W.C. Field died in 1946.

The Cenozoic Era started 65 million years ago and extends to the present. The apatosaurus lived during the Paleozoic Era (600 million to 225 million years ago.)

Suspect 2—Beecham Ness
The Longitude of Hackensack, New Jersey, is approximately 74 degrees west.

D.W. Griffith died in 1948.

Coelacanths are found in the western Indian Ocean, not off the coast of New Jersey.

Suspect 3—Beauregard Ness
The latitude of Atlantic City is approximately 40 degrees north.

Al Jolson died in 1950.

Sonar uses sound waves, not infrared light.

Suspect 4—Billy Ness
The Greatest Show On Earth won the Academy Award for best motion picture in 1952.

Lungfish are freshwater fish found in Africa, Australia, and South America.

The Mystery of the Blistered Ballerina

The Crime

Maria Nutcashova was a legend in her own time. The prima ballerina had danced with Nureyev, Villella, Baryshnikov, and all the other leading danseurs of the past quarter-century. She had sparkled in *The Nutcracker Suite*, left people breathless in *La Gypsy*, and wrenched their hearts with her interpretation of *Giselle*. No wonder people were paying extravagant prices to see her performance of *Swan Lake* at the New World Civic Center.

Unfortunately, those people never got the chance to see Maria Nutcashova dance. On the day of the performance, she was awakened by an agonizing itching on her feet. They were covered with watery blisters that her podiatrist husband diagnosed as poison ivy.

The Problem

Who caused the ballerina's case of poison ivy?

The Suspects

Suspect 1: Maria Nutcashova

Maria Nutcashova, prima ballerina, was born in Cherbourg, France, near the English Channel, the year Vaslav Nijinsky died.

"I have danced all of the most famous ballets," Maria Nutcashova told us. "From Igor Stravinsky's *Firebird* to Sergei Prokofiev's *Romeo and Juliet*, and yet..."

"I was frightened by this performance," she admitted honestly. "*Swan Lake* is one of the most desirable roles for a ballerina because the choreography is so spectacular for the women dancers. But, it is a physically demanding ballet. My anxiety caused me to suffer from depression, but then I pulled myself together. I reminded myself that the great genius Peter Tchaikovsky suffered from long bouts of depression, but it was during those depressions that he wrote his most cheerful music. I decided to face my fears and show the world that Maria Nutcashova was still a superlative performer."

Maria Nutcashova's alibi: "I had difficulty with my *tour en l'air* at the rehearsal, and I'm afraid that I broke down in tears. But, when I got home, I put on my ballet slippers and practiced my exercises at the barre. When one falls from a horse, one must climb back on immediately. Is that not so?"

Suspect 2: Sugar Plumb

Sugar Plumb, a ballerina, was born in Genoa, Italy, which is on the coast of the Ligurian Sea, the year Twyla Tharp choreographed "Eight Jelly Rolls." Because she was Maria Nutcashova's understudy, Sugar Plumb danced the lead role in the performance of *Swan Lake*.

"It was exciting," Sugar Plumb admitted. "To hear the applause and know it was for me; that is something a ballerina longs for and only a lucky few receive. Maria Nutcashova's misfortune was the start of my career."

"And, her misfortune saved the entire company from embarrassment," Sugar Plumb continued. "She may have been a great ballerina in her day, but she is too old and twenty pounds too heavy now. Her right arm no longer curves gracefully above her head in the third position, her leg shakes when she leans forward into the *arabesque allongee,* her *entrechat* does not have enough height to be effective. And, her *tour en l'air* ... well, even she herself knew she was incapable of making a complete turn in the air when she sprang up. She burst into tears and rushed to her dressing room when she muffed the step during the rehearsal."

Sugar Plumb's alibi: "Maria Nutcashova left the stage so suddenly she forgot to take her extra pair of ballet slippers with her. I took them to her dressing room. She is no longer a great ballerina, but she deserves my respect and sympathy. After all, I may be like her someday."

Suspect 3: Guy Hooph

Guy Hooph, the choreographer, was born in Corpus Christi, Texas, on the shores of the Gulf of Mexico, the year Edward Villella joined the New York City Ballet.

"It was a disaster," Guy Hooph admitted honestly. "Tchaikovsky's *Swan Lake* requires more spins than any other classical ballet. Maria Nutcashova no longer possessed the stamina to dance it, but she wouldn't admit that to herself. She insisted on going through with the performance."

"A ballerina's life is hard," Guy Hooph said sympathetically. "It begins before the age of twenty and is usually over by the age of 45. Mikhail Baryshnikov is six years younger than Maria, but he has had the good sense to broaden his career options. He has appeared in several movies and has choreographed versions of *The Nutcracker* and *Don Quixote*. I tried telling Maria that she should find another outlet for her creative energies, but she wouldn't listen. It is hard for a woman like her to give up the applause and the adoration that comes with being a prima ballerina."

Guy Hooph's alibi: "I followed Maria Nutcashova to her dressing room to try to talk sense to her one more time. While I was there, Sugar Plumb appeared at the door with Maria's dancing slippers. I put them on Maria's dressing table."

Suspect 4: Dr. Juan Miguel Huella

Dr. Juan Miguel Huella, Maria's husband, was born in Alicante, Spain, on the shores of the Mediterranean Sea, ten years after Anna Pavlova died.

"Maria was suffering from an acute irritation caused by exposure of the skin of her feet to the oil of the *Rhus vernix* plant. That is, poison ivy to the layman," Dr. Huella explained. "It is a common North American plant. We have some of it in the field behind our house. The oil is extremely poisonous, somewhat like acetic acid. However, the damage is temporary. She could have sustained far more serious injuries if she had danced *Swan Lake*."

"The foot is a complicated mechanism," Dr. Huella continued to explain. "It contains 36 bones, all held together in two arches by a system of ligaments. The foot is designed to act as a shock absorber for the leg, but no foot was designed to withstand the punishment of dancing *sur les pointes*. That position is totally unnatural for the body."

Dr. Juan Miguel Huella's alibi: "When Maria came home I saw how exhausted she was, so I tried to talk her out of the performance. But, she wouldn't listen to reason. Maria does what Maria chooses to do. She has always been that way, and I know from experience that arguing won't change her mind. At least I was able to convince her to relax and have a cup of herb tea before she donned her slippers and practiced at the barre."

The Mystery of the Blistered Ballerina

The Solution

"Maria does what Maria chooses to do." Maria's husband knew from long experience that Maria Nutcashova would dance the demanding *Swan Lake* ballet, even if that meant risking permanent damage to her feet. Because he could not reason with her, he decided to let the *Rhus radicans* plant do the reasoning for him. While the tea was brewing, he slipped out to the field behind their house and picked a few juicy leaves of the topical poison (taking care to wear gloves so he would not contract poison ivy himself). He rubbed the leaves inside her ballet slippers, knowing that she intended to put them on and practice at the barre. Because the oil takes time to penetrate and irritate the skin, the blisters did not appear until the following morning.

Information about the suspect

Suspect 1—Maria Nutcashova

Cherboug, France, is near the English Channel.

Vaslav Nijinsky died in 1950.

Igor Stravinsky wrote the music for *Firebird*.

Sergei Prokofiev wrote the music for *Romeo and Juliet*.

Swan Lake is one of the most desirable roles for a ballerina because the choreography is so spectacular for the women dancers.

Peter Tchaikovsky suffered from long bouts of depression, during which he wrote his most cheerful music.

Suspect 2—Sugar Plumb

Genoa, Italy, is on the coast of the Ligurian Sea.

Twyla Tharp choreographed "Eight Jelly Rolls" in 1971.

In the third ballet position, the right arm is supposed to curve gracefully above the head.

In an *arabesque allongee*, one leg is raised while the dancer leans forward.

An *entrechat* is a jump straight up, during which the dancer rapidly crosses and uncrosses his or her legs.

A *tour en l'air* is a complete turn in the air after the dancer springs up.

Suspect 3—Guy Hooph

Corpus Christi, Texas, is on the shores of the Gulf of Mexico.

Edward Villella joined the New York City Ballet in 1957.

Tchaikovsky's *Swan Lake* requires more spins than any other classical ballet.

A ballerina's career usually begins before the age of twenty and is over by the age of 45.

Mikhail Baryshnikov is six years younger than Maria Nutcashova. (She was born in 1942. He was born in 1948.)

Baryshnikov has appeared in several movies and has choreographed versions of *The Nutcracker* and *Don Quixote*.

Suspect 4—Dr. Juan Miguel Huella

Alicante, Spain, is on the shores of the Mediterranean Sea.

Anna Pavlova died in 1931. Dr. Huella was born ten years later in 1941.

The poison ivy plant is classified as *Rhus radicans*, not *Rhus vernix*.

Poison ivy oil is extremely poisonous, but it resembles carbolic acid. Acetic acid is the acid found in vinegar.

The foot contains 26 bones and three arches, not 36 and two arches.

The foot is designed to act as a shock absorber for the leg.

Dr. Huella was right when he said that no foot was designed to withstand the punishment of dancing *sur les pointes* (on the toes). That position is totally unnatural for the body.

The Mystery of the Disappearing Dolphin

The Crime

Mimsi, a bottle-nosed dolphin, was Aqua-Park's most flamboyant attraction. She jumped through flaming hoops, used her mouth to catch and throw a ball, and snatched fish from her trainer's out-stretched hand. But, her most amazing feats involved her sense of echolocation.

The lagoon where Mimsi was housed was built with a simulated shipwreck on its floor. When Mimsi's trainer showed the dolphin a picture of an object, Mimsi would swim to the shipwreck and return with that item in her mouth. She was spectacular. She was brilliant. She was person-able. She was photogenic. And, one sad morning, she was missing.

"She was kidnapped," her trainer told us. "I warned the owner of Aqua-Park that we needed better security. Mimsi's lagoon was built ten feet from the ocean, with a six-foot-high retaining wall around it. It would have been possible for the thieves to bring a boat up to the shoreline, tranquilize Mimsi, and use a sling to lift her over the wall."

"I just hope she's all right," he added tear-fully, "wherever she is."

The Problem

Who caused Mimsi's disappearance?

The Suspects

Suspect 1: Rex Bagshaw

Rex Bagshaw, a salvor and treasure hunter, was born in Sunset, Utah, near the Great Salt Lake, the year that Jacques-Yves Cousteau wrote *World Without Sun*.

Rex owns a large boat outfitted with winches and slings. "It's for my business," Rex explained. "I make most of my money from the salvages of foundered vessels but I also scout around for wrecks of old Spanish ships that went down off the Florida Keys on their way home from the Spanish Main. Sometimes I find a few doubloons, like this one." He touched the round gold object that hung from the chain he wore around his neck.

"I'd like to find a really big shipwreck," he admitted, "something like the *Titanic* that went down in the North Atlantic in 1912. But, it's a big ocean. Finding a sunken ship takes a lot of luck and expensive sonar equipment."

Rex Bagshaw's alibi: "I just bought a little island that used to be a fish farm. I spend all of my spare time repairing the underwater pens that are connected to the dock."

Suspect 2: Ramona Sympatico

Ramona Sympatico, the president of GLAD (Give Living Animals Dignity), was born in Windsor Locks, Connecticut, near the Connecticut River, the year that Jane Goodall began her research in Tanzania.

GLAD is an animal rights group that opposes all forms of animal captivity. "Zoos are detestable examples of unjust incarceration," Ramona protested vehemently. "Consider gorillas. In their native African habitat, they are shy, friendly, quiet vegetarians. But, people didn't leave them alone.

People captured them and put them in cages for everyone to gawk at. The first few zoo gorillas died very quickly, probably from loneliness."

"Aqua-Park locks up dolphins and forces them to perform silly tricks," Ramona continued bitterly. "Mimsi wasn't happy there. I could tell that from her unhappy squeaks when she leaped high into the air and caught sight of the sunlight glistening off the ocean. The poor, sweet little creature. I asked the owner of Aqua-Park to let her go, but he just laughed at me."

Ramona Sympatico's alibi: "I was boating. I stayed out on the ocean until almost midnight because I was watching a large school of gray cetaceans who were following the coastline. I believe they were bottle-nosed dolphins or one of the other members of the whale family."

Suspect 3: Victor Tortolini

Victor Tortolini, owner of the Laughing Gull restaurant, was born in Kingston, on the West Indian island of Jamaica, the year *On the Waterfront* won the Academy Award for Best Motion Picture.

The Laughing Gull specializes in fresh seafood, especially queen conch, snapper, Florida pompano, and swordfish. The menu board outside the door advertises this disturbing offering:

TODAY'S SPECIAL – DOLPHIN.

"You bleeding heart dolphin lovers really annoy me," Victor snapped when we expressed our concern about his choice of victuals. "That Sympatico woman comes in here talking about the rights of dolphins while she stuffs her face with my double-decker hamburger special. She's all fired up about protecting one mammal, but she has no qualms about eating another. Give me a break! I'll tell you the same thing I told her: I know the difference between a mammal and a fish, and the dolphin on my grill is definitely a fish."

Victor Tortolini's alibi: "I went down to the docks because I heard that someone had caught a whale shark, which is the world's largest fish. But it was just a crazy rumor. Those fish are pretty rare."

Suspect 4: Mimsi

Mimsi, the bottle-nosed dolphin, could not be interviewed directly, but her trainer allowed us to listen to tapes of her click and whistle form of speech. The following translation was made of her last recorded communication:

"Mimsi born off coast of Barrow, Alaska. Many fish. Mimsi likes fish. Squid for breakfast tomorrow? First remember shipwreck. Big explosion, ship sink. Letters on side say M A I N E. Must be name of ship. Many two-legged animals can't swim."

"Mimsi caught in net. Struggle. Hard to breathe. Saved by pale two-legged animals. Brought here. Food good. Like squid. Lonely sometimes. Sometimes hear clicks of other Mimsies. Somewhere. Look but can't find friends. Squid for breakfast? Mimsi likes squid best. Eight arms on squid. Mimsi can count. One…Two…Three…"

"Mimsi hears something. Other Mimsies? No! Wait!" (Here Mimsi's phonations become very agitated.) "Stop! Help me! Wait!…."

The Solution

Mimsi wasn't very knowledgeable about geography or history, but she was in touch with her own feelings: she knew that she was lonely for others like herself. While Ramona Sympatico watched a school of gray cetaceans follow the coastline, Mimsi heard them calling out to one another in the click and whistle dialect of her own species.

"Help me!" she cried out to them, forgetting all about the squid she might get for breakfast if she stayed in her man-made lagoon. "Stop!" she cried, imploring them not to leave her behind as they swam off into the sea. Summoning all her courage, Mimsi leaped high into the air, rising easily above the six-foot wall and arching gracefully across the ten-foot strip of earth that separated her from a whole new life of freedom.

Information about the suspects

Suspect 1—Rex Bagshaw
Sunset, Utah, is near the Great Salt Lake.

Jacques-Yves Cousteau wrote *World Without Sun* in 1964.

The Spanish Main was the name given by pirates and English buccaneers to the northern coast of South America. Spanish ships on their way home from the Spanish Main sank in the waters near the Florida Keys in the 1500s.

A doubloon is an old Spanish gold coin.

The Titanic sank in the North Atlantic in 1912 after hitting an iceberg.

Suspect 2—Ramona Sympatico
Windsor Locks, Connecticut, is near the Connecticut River.

Jane Goodall began her chimpanzee research in Tanzania in 1960.

Gorillas are shy, friendly, quiet African animals that feed on leaves and fruit.

Some people think that the first gorillas in captivity died of loneliness.

Bottle-nosed dolphins are grey. They are cetaceans, which means they are closely related to whales.

Suspect 3—Victor Tortolini
Kingston is the capital of the West Indian island of Jamaica.

On the Waterfront won the Academy Award for Best Motion Picture in 1954.

Queen conch, snapper, Florida pompano, and swordfish are all edible seafoods that might be served in Florida restaurants.

The dorado fish is often called the dolphin fish. It is not the same as the bottle-nosed dolphin, which is a mammal.

The whale shark is the world's largest fish. It is rare.

Suspect 4—Mimsi
Bottle-nosed dolphins live in warm or tropical waters. Barrow, Alaska, on the Arctic Ocean, is too cold for bottle-nosed dolphins.

The *Maine* sank in 1898. Because dolphins probably live for 25 to 50years, it is impossible for Mimsi to have witnessed the sinking of the *Maine*.

Squid have ten arms, not eight.

Dolphins do like squid. Mimsi was telling the truth about that.

The Mystery of the Heisted Hymenoptera

The Crime

"She had three pairs of legs, five eyes, and a long tongue that hung from the outside of her head, but she was beautiful to me," Jason Buswell told us as he led us across the clover-covered lawn to the scene of the crime.

"I procured the queen bee and her workers from the Agricultural School at the University of Minnesota. Now, someone has stolen the queen," he complained, opening the boxlike hive and pulling out the drawer that contained the brood chamber. "She used to be right here, and now she's gone. I know she didn't die because I didn't find her body. Someone stole my hymenoptera, and I'd like to know why."

The Problem

Who stole Jason Buswell's queen bee?

The Suspects

Suspect 1

Buzz Crenshaw, a beekeeper, was born in Devils Lake, North Dakota, which is west of Grand Forks, the year BeBe Shopp won the Miss America Contest.

"I didn't steal his darned queen bee!" Buzz Crenshaw answered our question with a derisive laugh. "He's been spreading the story that his bees were a new hybrid strain that could produce better honey, but let me tell you, kid, a honeybee is a honeybee. The quality of their honey depends on what they eat—pure and simple. Look at that jar on the shelf." He pointed to a jar of amber-colored honey. "That honey came from aster and goldenrod nectar. You'd get an almost white honey if your bees were feeding on orange blossoms, but we don't have orange blossoms here in Minnesota."

"Jason Buswell annoyed me," Buzz Crenshaw admitted. "His bragging about his new bees and their new methods for making quality honey implied that my honey wasn't first-rate. Hey, it's all the same stuff—regurgitated nectar and bee enzymes with the water evaporated out."

Buzz Crenshaw's alibi: "I took my wife to the doctor because she had a bad case of hives."

Suspect 2

Beau Beal, a neighborhood child, was born in Huatabampo, Mexico, near the Gulf of California, the year *Wind Beneath My Wings* by Bette Midler won the Grammy Award for Best Record.

"I've got an insect collection. Want to see it?" Beau asked eagerly, as he led us into his chaotic bedroom. "I've got my specimens organized in order of their taxonomic order. See, here's a tray of Odonata. The biggest member of this family is the Megaloprepus caeruleata. My father's going to try to find me one the next time he goes on a business trip to South America."

"And, here's a tray of Orthoptera. They're real easy to find around here. Minnesota's got lots of crickets and grasshoppers, and I find the roaches behind the Burger-Easy restaurant."

We asked to see his collection of Hymenoptera. "Hymenoptera? Oh…" Beau squinted as he surveyed the debris that lay jumbled on all his bedroom shelves. "I don't know where my Hymenoptera tray is. I suppose I could find it if I cleaned things up a bit. Could you come back tomorrow?"

Beau Beal's alibi: "I was catching bee flies. They look like bees, but they're in the order Diptera with true flies."

Suspect 3: Beatrice Fuzzlake

Beatrice Fuzzlake, Jason Buswell's neighbor, was born in Bountiful, Utah, near the Great Salt Lake, the year William Beebe died.

"I hate bees!" Beatrice Fuzzlake told us vehemently. "I am so deathly allergic to them that I have to garden in a beekeeper's hat and gloves just to keep from being stung. It was bad enough that Buzz Crenshaw kept bees, but now Jason Buswell has brought in a new strain of the insect. You know what they are, don't you? Killer bees!"

"A Mexican scientist developed them, but they got loose and now they're spreading through the United States. They don't swarm like regular bees do, but their venom is so potent one sting can kill a horse! I lived in fear that one of them was going to get me. But, now that the queen is gone, the hive will die. Thank God for that!"

Beatrice Fuzzlake's alibi: "I was inside my house reading Shakespeare's famous soliloquy from Hamlet. 'To be, or not to be...'"

Suspect 4: Blossom Beech

Blossom Beech, a jewelry maker, was born in Winona, Minnesota, near the Minnesota-Wisconsin border, the year *The Sting* won the Academy Award for Best Motion Picture.

"I make simulated fossil jewelry," Blossom told us. "My plastic trilobite bracelets sold pretty well, but my biggest seller is my insect-in-amber necklaces. Real amber was sap from maple trees that got buried and hardened into fossils. But, real amber is expensive, so I make my own amber out of brownish-yellow plastic."

"At first I was putting ants in the simulated amber. Then, I did some bee-in-amber necklaces, and people went crazy for them, even though bees weren't around back when fossils were made. I guess bees are more chic than ants, and I can get a lot of them in my Aunt Beatrice's garden."

Blossom Beech's alibi: "I was in my studio experimenting with a new caterpillar-in-amber design."

The Solution

If ordinary bees in amber sold well, imagine how much more money Blossom Beech could get for a queen-bee-in-amber necklace. Maybe she got the idea of stealing Jason Buswell's queen bee from her aunt's hysterical complaints about the hive of killer bees next door, or maybe her aunt suggested it directly: "I've got a beekeeper's hat and gloves. Why don't you put them on and steal the queen bee out of Buswell's hive?" Whoever had the idea, two facts are certain—they were in it together, and Blossom did the actual stealing. It is unlikely that Beatrice Fuzzlake would have gone anywhere near a hive that she suspected to be full of killer bees. Beatrice must have been dismayed when she later learned that stealing the queen bee does not kill a hive. The workers simply hatch a few more queens.

Information about the suspects

Suspect 1—Buzz Crenshaw

Devils Lake, North Dakota, is west of Grand Forks, North Dakota.

BeBe Shopp won the Miss America Contest in 1948.

The quality of honey largely depends on what bees eat. A diet of aster and goldenrod nectar produces a dark amber-colored honey.

Orange blossom nectar produces an almost white honey.

Orange trees require a warmer climate than Minnesota's.

To make honey, bees regurgitate nectar from their nectar stomachs into wax cells, add bee enzymes, and let the water in the nectar evaporate.

Suspect 2—Beau Beal

Huatabampo, Mexico, is near the Gulf of California.

Wind Beneath My Wings by Bette Midler won the Grammy Award for Best Record in 1989.

The order Orthoptera includes crickets, grasshoppers, and roaches, all of which can be found in Minnesota.

The bee fly looks like a bee, but it is in the order Diptera with the true flies.

Suspect 3—Beatrice Fuzzlake

Bountiful, Utah, is near the Great Salt Lake.

William Beebe died in 1962.

It is possible to be so allergic to bee stings that the result of a sting is death.

A Brazilian scientist developed killer bees.

Killer bees are capable of killing animals and people because they attack in swarms.

A beehive does not usually die when the queen is removed. Workers feed royal jelly to several larvae to create new queens.

William Shakespeare wrote Hamlet.

Suspect 4—Blossom Beech

Winona, Minnesota, is near the Minnesota-Wisconsin border.

The Sting won the Academy Award for Best Motion Picture in 1973.

Real amber was the fossilized sap from pine trees, not maple trees.

Fossil bees found trapped in amber probably lived 50 million years ago.

The Mystery of the Incinerated Schoolhouse

The Crime

It started in the boiler room. A spark fell into a pile of oily rags, and the rags burst into flame. Within minutes, thick black smoke was pouring from the windows of the old wooden schoolhouse that dated back to 1916.

Fortunately, the fire had ignited just as the last busload of students was pulling out of the parking lot. No one was injured, but the school burned to the ground, taking all the social studies and mathematics textbooks with it.

"It could have been arson," the fire chief admitted later as his men hosed down the smoldering remains. "But, I don't know what kind of lunatic would be depraved enough to burn down a school."

The Problem

Who burned down the school?

The Suspect

Suspect 1: Jackie Blase

Jackie Blase, a student, was born in Aurora, which is in the southwestern corner of Missouri, the year Manuel Noriega of Panama surrendered to U.S. troops.

Jackie Blase wants to be a firefighter when she grows up. "My mom's dead set against it," she admitted. "Firefighting is one of the most dangerous occupations in this country. But, I just love fires. I used to want to work on the ladder trucks because that's the truck that carries all the really nifty tools, but lately I've been thinking it would be fun to run the pumper truck. That's the truck that hooks up to the water hydrant and puts extra pressure on the water so it can be squirted farther."

"But, I'd really like to work at an airport," she told us in an excited voice. "The fire appliance with the greatest pumping capacity is used to put out aircraft fires. It's the 860-horsepower eight-wheel Oshkosh fire truck, which pumps foam. It's totally awesome."

Jackie Blase's alibi: "I was supposed to be on the bus, but I wasn't," Jackie admitted. "My parents don't get home until five o'clock, and it's lonely at home. So, sometimes I hang around the playground after school and then walk home. My mom doesn't care."

Suspect 2: Edna Fry

Edna Fry, a teacher, was born in Homer, Alaska, near Cook Inlet, the year Dr. Albert Bruce Sabin developed a live-virus vaccine for poliomyelitis.

"Are you old enough to remember poliomyelitis?" Miss Fry demanded in her most intimidating schoolteacher's voice. "It was a terrifying disease that killed children and left many of the survivors paralyzed. It attacks and kills muscle cells, especially the muscle cells in the legs. That's what happened to my brother Larry, and it happened to Franklin Delano Roosevelt, too, when he was ten years old. Then, Dr. Edmond Salk, God bless him, developed a vaccine."

"Well, this fire was a vaccine, too. The schoolhouse was a firetrap just waiting for a tragedy to happen, but the school committee wouldn't tear it down and build a new one. Oh, no, that would cost money, and we can't spend the town's money on anything as frivolous as safety for our children," Miss Fry continued bitterly. "But, now we have to. The fire was just like a vaccine of weaker germs that forces the body to make antibodies against a stronger strain of the same germ. Because the fire occurred when all the children were out of the building, no one died. Now, the town will be forced to build a safer school. If it was arson, then I say let's give the arsonist a medal."

Edna Fry's alibi: "I was tidying up the teacher's lounge. There were scuff marks on the coffee table, and I was trying to remove them with a little gasoline on a rag. I smelled the smoke and had onlyenough time to pull the fire alarm before I ran from the building."

Suspect 3: Harold Washburn

Harold Washburn, the custodian, was born in Las Animas, Colorado, near the Arkansas River, the year the Cocoanut Grove Fire claimed 491 lives.

"The thing that hurts most is that my good soap-making kettle got crushed under the debris in the boiler room," Harold Washburn told us. "I had to make my own soap because the school committee didn't give me enough money to buy the cleaning supplies I needed. It's not too hard, though. You put some kind of fat, either animal or vegetable fat, into a big kettle. Add some lye, and simmer it over a bunsen burner for several hours. Then, sprinkle salt on the top. The 'neat soap' rises to the top. You skim that off and let it harden. It makes a good, long-lasting soap, although it does tend to form a soap curd when it reacts with minerals in hard water."

Harold Washburn's alibi: "I had just set a fresh pot of lard and alkali on to simmer in the boiler room. Then, I went down the corridor to empty wastebaskets. When I heard the fire alarm I ran like holy heck to get out of the building. You weren't going to catch me hanging around in that tinderbox."

Suspect 4: Peter Gog

Peter Gog, a teacher, was born in Beijing, which used to be called Peking, China.

Beijing is west of Dandong, China. He was born the year the U.S. government passed a law requiring a health warning on every pack of cigarettes.

"I'm really nervous today," Peter Gog admitted. "I'm trying to quit smoking. It's a filthy, expensive habit, but I'm afraid that I'm addicted. I started smoking in China, which is the world's leading producer of tobacco, and I smoked all through college. I like the way small amounts of nicotine stimulated my heart and made it beat a little faster. But, nicotine in large, concentrated amounts is a poison," Peter Gog admitted as he unwrapped a stick of gum and stuffed it in his mouth. "The Puritans in America had the right idea. They considered tobacco a dangerous narcotic."

Peter Gog's alibi: "Well, I hate to admit this," Peter Gog said sheepishly. "But, right after school I ducked into the boiler room to sneak a fast cigarette. Then, I left the building. I was in my car when I heard the fire alarm ring."

The Solution

It was a busy boiler room. Harold Washburn had just mixed up a kettle of soap soup and Peter Gog had ducked in for a fast fix of nicotine, but Edna Fry was able to find a moment to run in with a gasoline-soaked rag. Touching it quickly to the flame of the bunsen burner, she tossed it into the corner, waiting only a few seconds to make sure it touched off a roaring blaze. Then, she beat a fast retreat, remembering to pull the fire alarm on her way out of the building.

Miss Fry set the fire for altruistic reasons (to prevent a fire when children were in the building and to force the town to build a new, safer school). She was so concerned with the safety of children, however, that she didn't realize she was endangering adults. Harold Washburn was still in the building emptying wastebaskets. Peter Gog might have gone back to his classroom instead of to his car. Even Jackie Blase, who was reluctant to go home to an empty house, might have slipped back into the school. It was a terribly misguided solution to a difficult problem, but Miss Fry will probably get away with it. Only one percent of all arson cases end in a conviction.

Information about the suspects

Suspect 1—Jackie Blase
Aurora is in the southwestern corner of Missouri.

Manuel Noriega of Panama surrendered to U.S. troops in 1990.

Fire fighting is one of the most dangerous occupations in this country.

Ladder trucks carry most of the fire-fighting tools.

The pumper truck hooks up to the water hydrant and puts extra pressure on the water so it can be squirted farther.

The fire appliance with the greatest pumping capacity is the 860-horsepower eight-wheel Oshkosh fire truck, which puts out aircraft and runway fires. It pumps foam.

Suspect 2—Edna Fry
Homer, Alaska, is near Cook Inlet.

Dr. Albert Bruce Sabin developed a live-virus vaccine for poliomyelitis in 1960.

Poliomyelitis attacks the nerve cells of the brain and spinal cord, not muscle cells.

Franklin Delano Roosevelt contracted polio when he was 39 years old.

Dr. Salk's name is Jonas Edward Salk, not Edmond Salk.

Some vaccines are strains of weaker germs that force the body to make antibodies against a stronger strain of the same germ.

Suspect 3—Harold Washburn
Las Animas, Colorado, is near the Arkansas River.

The Cocoanut Grove Fire claimed 491 lives in 1942.

Soap is made by heating animal or vegetable fat with lye, then adding salt to make the neat soap rise to the top, where it can be skimmed off for hardening.

Lard is animal fat. Lye is an alkali.

Suspect 4—Peter Gog
Beijing, China, used to be called Peking.

Beijing is west of Dandong, China.

The Mystery of the Incinerated Schoolhouse

The U.S government passed a law requiring a health warning on every pack of cigarettes in 1966.

China is the world's leading producer of tobacco.

Small amounts of nicotine stimulate the heart.

Nicotine in large, concentrated amounts is a poison.

The Puritans in America considered tobacco a dangerous narcotic.

The Mystery of the Purloined Pumpkin

The Crime

On October 15, Leroy Gardner made his way out to his pumpkin patch to pick and weigh what he was sure would be the largest pumpkin grown in the county that year. But, where he should have seen a large orange orb shining like a fallen harvest moon, he found only trampled leaves, tangled vines, and a rut where the enormous vegetable had been rolled away. The trail ended at the macadam, rain-washed street.

Leroy had mulched and watered and fertilized and sung to the pumpkin all summer long. Now, someone had stolen his prize gourd one day before the county fair's monster pumpkin contest.

The Problem

Who stole Leroy's pumpkin?

The Suspects

Suspect 1: Silas Marinara

Silas Marinara, a neighbor and rival pumpkin grower, was born in Euclid, Ohio, near Lake Erie, the year that *How Green Was My Valley* won the Academy Award for best motion picture.

"I didn't need to steal Leroy Gardner's pumpkin," Silas Marinara told us sharply. "My pumpkin's bigger than his pumpkin, and I didn't have to sing to it to get it that big, either. I grew it with good old-fashioned common sense. Look at this one," he invited, leading us through the garden to a vegetable that looked large enough to hold Peter Pumpkin-Eater's diminutive wife. "Pumpkins are related to squash. Most of them weigh between 15 to 30 pounds, but the biggest pumpkin ever grown weighed more than 600 pounds. All you have to remember is that they like slightly acid soil and only the female flowers produce pumpkins."

Silas Marinara's alibi: "I was reading a booklet from the county agricultural service on how to kill Japanese beetles. Those things have been a garden pest ever since they came to this country around 1916."

Suspect 2: The Goon Gang

The Goon Gang—a group of neighborhood children named Lonnie, Donnie, Ronnie, Connie, Fawn, and Sqweegie— were all born in Farmington, New Hampshire, on the banks of the Cocheco River, three years after Christa McAuliffe died in space.

October means only one thing to the Goon Gang—Halloween. They know everything there is to know about the holiday, from its origins as a Celtic New Year's Eve celebration in honor of Samhain, the Celtic lord of death, to the Irish parade in honor of Muck Olla. They know about the English custom of going a-souling to beg for soulcakes. But, their favorite story is the old Irish legend about Jack, the man who could enter neither heaven nor hell. "He has to wander the earth carrying a lantern until Judgement Day," Donnie informed us.

"The story of Jack's lantern led to the custom of carving jack-o'-lanterns on Halloween," Connie added. "We wanted to carve a really big jack-o'-lantern this year, but we didn't have enough money to buy a pumpkin."

The Goon Gang's alibi: "We didn't steal the pumpkin. We couldn't have because we were... uh ... sort of like... stealing apples off Mr. Marinara's apple trees that night." "They were Granny Smiths," Donnie elaborated. "They were green and very tart."

Suspect 3: Lydia Rose

Lydia Rose, a neighbor and 4-H Club leader, was born in Wewoka, Oklahoma, south of Ponca City, the year John Steinbeck wrote *Cannery Row.*

"I've been a 4-H Club leader for years and years," Mrs. Rose told us cheerfully as she puttered around her fragrant kitchen. "The four H's stand for health, happiness, helpfulness, and handicraft, and I believe in every one of those goals completely. Because three-quarters of our members live on farms, the 4-H organization performs a very important social function for our young people. That's why I'm happy to help."

"Although I bit off a little more than I could chew when I offered to make 50 pumpkin pies for the 4-H bake sale table at the county fair," Lydia Rose admitted, "I ran out of ingredients halfway through the baking and was in a state of panic. My husband Arthur, bless his heart, drove all the way to Portsmouth to buy a case of pumpkin pie filling. Ordinarily, I wouldn't use canned ingredients in my pies, but at that point I was desperate enough to do anything."

Lydia Rose's alibi: "I was right here in my kitchen all night, slicing and chopping and boiling and mashing the ingredients for the pies."

Suspect 4: Lucy Gardner

Lucy Gardner, Leroy Gardner's wife, was born in Loveland, Colorado, west of Fort Morgan, the year Fritz Kreisler died.

"I have had it up to here with that pumpkin," Lucy Gardner snapped as she drew her finger across her forehead. "Leroy had a crazy notion that music would affect the way it grew, so he used to serenade it with the lute. He'd sit out there for hours, strumming his fingers across the eleven strings of the instrument, singing love songs appassionato. The love songs he used to sing to me," she added, aggrieved, "he was singing those same lyrics to a vegetable!"

"But, the last straw came when he decided to put wheels on my antique celesta so he could wheel that out into the garden, too. He claimed that its clear, sweet tones would soothe the pumpkin and make it grow more uniformly round. That instrument was designed by Auguste Mustel in 1886. I was not about to have it used as a gardening tool."

Lucy Gardner's alibi: "I was on the phone to my lawyer."

The Mystery of the Purloined Pumpkin

The Solution

Lydia Rose gave herself away when she said she was in her kitchen "slicing and chopping and boiling and mashing the ingredients for the pies." Canned pumpkin pie filling is already cooked and pureed.

When she ran out of ingredients for the 50 pumpkin pies she had agreed to make, Lydia Rose became desperate enough to steal Leroy Gardner's pumpkin. She cut it off the vine with her paring knife and rolled it home. (Maybe her husband, Arthur, bless his heart, helped her.) Then, she chopped up the evidence of her crime and poured it into pie shells.

Information about the suspects

Suspect 1—Silas Marinara
Euclid, Ohio, is near Lake Erie.

How Green Was My Valley won the Academy Award for best motion picture in 1941.

Most pumpkins weigh between 15 and 30 pounds, but the largest recorded weight for a pumpkin is well over 600 pounds.

Pumpkins like slightly acid soil.

Only female flowers produce pumpkins.

Japanese beetles came to this country about 1916.

Suspect 2—The Goon Gang
Farmington, New Hampshire, is on the banks of the Cocheco River.

Christa McAuliffe died aboard the *Challenger* in 1986. The Goon Gang members were born three years later, in 1989.

The Celtic New Year's Eve celebration in honor of Samhain, the Celtic lord of death, is one of the origins of Halloween.

The Irish used to have parades honoring the god Muck Olla.

The English used to go a-souling (begging) for soulcakes (pastry given in return for the promise to pray for the dead).

According to Irish legend, Jack must wander the earth with a lantern until Judgement Day.

Granny Smith apples are green and tart.

Suspect 3—Lydia Rose
Wewoka, Oklahoma, is south of Ponca City, Oklahoma.

John Steinbeck wrote *Cannery Row* in 1945.

The 4-H club's four H's stand for head, heart, hands and health.

Suspect 4—Lucy Gardner
Loveland, Colorado, is west of Fort Morgan, Colorado.

Fitz Kreisler died in 1962.

The lute is a pear-shaped instrument with eleven strings.

Appassionato is a musical term which means "with great feeling."

The celesta is a pianolike instrument with clear, sweet tones.

The celesta was designed by Auguste Mustel in 1886.

The Mystery of the Sabotaged Salad

The Crime

La Maison de Ratatouille was the ritziest restaurant in the city. The house specialty, braised sweetbreads in olive sauce, was piquant. The avocado and watercress soup was refreshingly tart. The salmon in green aspic was a subtle delicacy. The bill was astronomical. "My food is worth every penny of the price," Chef Henri was fond of saying. "I defy anyone to find fault with anything that is served at La Maison de Ratatouille."

Unfortunately, Roland Finick, the food critic for the largest newspaper in the city, didn't have to look far to find fault. Staring up at him from his salad bowl was a cockroach the size of a large pitted prune. He wrote a scathing review of the restaurant, suggesting that the Board of Health should close it down.

"I am ruined!" Chef Henri sobbed piteously. "Who could have hated me enough to sabotage my business?"

The Problem

Who put the cockroach in the salad?

The Suspects

Suspect 1: Madame Narcissa de Chat

Madame Narcissa de Chat, Chef Henri's former wife, was born in Port-au-Prince, the capital city of Haiti, the year that Francois Duvalier was elected president for life.

"Henri must be totally humiliated," Madam de Chat smiled maliciously as she filed her long red nails. "Though I doubt he is as humiliated as I was when I had to appear at Cannes in the same clothes I wore last year. Despite the fortune he was making in his restaurant, Henri refused to increase my alimony payments."

"I warned him not to refuse my demands," Madame de Chat continued in a voice that held absolutely no compassion. "I have been studying the voodoo rituals of my homeland. When Narcissa de Chat is angered, the spirits are angered. Henri is fortunate that retribution was as benign as a cockroach in a salad. Perhaps he will take my requests more seriously next time."

Narcissa de Chat's alibi: "I was in the restaurant that evening," she admitted with a shrug. "But, I was far too busy chatting with my attractive escort, a famous Italian movie producer, to pay attention to anything else that was happening in the room." I was telling Antonio that Christopher Columbus landed in Hispaniola in 1492 and established a base in what is now the country of Haiti.

Suspect 2: Jean de Chat

Jean de Chat, the son of Henri and Narcissa de Chat, was born in Yuba City, California, northeast of San Francisco, the year *Dances With Wolves* won the Academy Award for Best Motion Picture.

Jean is not a model of exemplary deportment. When wheedling and importuning do not get him what he wants, he resorts to conniption fits. His most annoying trait, however, is his penchant for practical jokes. He has put chattering teeth in his mother's jewelry box, whoopie cushions on the chairs at elegant dinner parties, and salt in the sugar bowl at the breakfast table. Chef Henri hopes that his son will someday follow in his culinary footsteps.

"No way, José!" Jean squealed as he hurled himself into a nearby chair. "I ain't cooking food for dumb nuts to eat, no way! I'm going to be an entymologist. Do you like my scorpion?" he asked, dropping the creature on the table. "My Mom said I couldn't keep any insects in the house, so I bought this instead. You can hold him, if you want to. Even if it stings you, you probably won't die."

Jean de Chat's alibi: "Yeah, I was in the restaurant that night," he admitted sullenly. "I wanted to show my new scorpion to someone. But, my dad was too busy rearranging lettuce leaves in a salad, and my mom was making googly eyes at some smarmy guy who was wearing more jewelry than she was. I thought about dropping the scorpion down his neck, but I was afraid the guy would kill it."

"Then someone started screaming about finding a bug in his food," Jean added with delight. "It was a big monster cockroach with bright colors, like you'd find in tropical rain forests. I asked if I could have it for my collection, but the man said he was keeping it for evidence. He wasn't very nice about it, either."

Suspect 3: Perin Arnaud

Perin Arnaud, the headwaiter at La Maison de Ratatouille, was born in Casablanca, on the coast of Morocco, Africa, the year that Irene Joilot-Curie died.

"The cockroach incident was most unfortunate," Mr. Arnaud admitted. "But, it is to be expected when the hoi polloi are admitted to an establishment like this. What can you expect from people who don't know the first thing about gourmet dining? These are the kind of people who order sturgeon eggs thinking it is caviar. They do not understand that the only caviar acceptable to an epicure is whitefish roe, and since Finland is the world's leading producer of good caviar, the delicacy is very expensive. They do not even know the difference between a truffle and trifle. Mon Dieu! I told Monsieur Henri de Chat that we should restrict the clientele to those who could properly appreciate what La Maison de Ratatouille has to offer. He did not agree. Since we had such disparate opinions on this matter, I have chosen to look elsewhere for employment."

Henri had a different version of their dissension. "If a customer slipped Perin Arnaud a twenty-dollar bill, he would be shown to a table. If he did not, he'd wait two, three, sometimes four hours before he would be seated. I ordered Arnaud to stop taking bribes, but I noticed that Bert Baker slipped something into his hand and was seated immediately. I was forced to rebuke Arnaud again."

Perin Arnaud's alibi: "I was with a very difficult patron, trying to explain to him that our truffle soup is made from the world's finest fungi, which, as you undoubtedly know, grow along the bark on oak tree branches. I was so busy I had time to give only a cursory glance at the tray that was taken to Monsieur Finick's table. I overlooked the vermin in the salad. Mon Dieu! How can I ever forgive myself for such a monumental lapse?"

Suspect 4: Bert Baker

Bert Baker, also known as "Mr. Beef," is the owner of Mr. Beef's Burgertown Bonanza, the largest and most successful restaurant in the city. He was born in Whitefish, Montana, southwest of Waterton Glacier International Peace Park, which is sometimes called Glacier National Park, the year Clarence Birdseye died.

"Look, I don't want this information to get around," Mr. Beef said, lowering his voice conspiratorially. "I'm the major investor in a new haute cuisine joint that's scheduled to open next week and Perin Arnaud has already agreed to come to work for me. It's a risky proposition, especially in a city that already has a pricey restaurant like La Maison de Ratatouille. But, I figured that if the Frenchman could make a go of it, then so could I. Of course, Finick's review can make or break a place like that, and he's never quite forgiven me for the case of typhoid fever he says he caught at my Burgertown Bonanza. He's crazy, of course. You can't catch typhoid fever from contaminated food."

Bert "Mr. Beef" Baker's alibi: "I was eating at La Maison de Ratatouille when the cockroach scandal happened. When Roland Finick started screaming, I strolled over to his table to check out the situation. The thing in his salad was certainly a cockroach. No doubt about it."

"I happen to know a thing or two about cockroaches," Mr. Beef admitted. "There are about 300 different kinds, and they're a real problem for restaurants because they like the cold, dark environment of restaurant refrigerators. We find cockroaches in our crates of bananas, but our staff is careful not to let our customers see any of them. It's a tough piece of luck for old Henri," Mr. Beef shrugged philosophically. "Roland Finick's review has really cost him business."

The Solution

Bert "Mr. Beef" Baker didn't slip Perin Arnaud a twenty-dollar bill for the privilege of being seated immediately at La Maison de Ratatouille. He slipped him a small case containing a tropical cockroach. (Jean de Chat said it was a tropical rain forest cockroach, and Jean de Chat is something of an expert in these matters.) Mr. Beef probably found the cockroach at Mr. Beef's Burgertown Bonanza in a crate of tropical bananas. With his own haute cuisine restaurant due to open soon, he saw a way to drive customers away from Henri's restaurant and into his.

More customers at Mr. Beef's new restaurant meant more opportunities for Perin Arnaud to take bribes. If Arnaud had any qualms at all about his role in sabotaging Henri de Chat's business, he probably overcame them when Henri scolded him for taking a bribe from a customer.

Information about the suspects

Suspect 1—Madame Narcissa de Chat
Port-au-Prince is the capital of Haiti.

Francois Duvalier arranged to be elected president for life in 1964.

Voodoo is practiced in Haiti.

Christopher Columbus landed on Hispaniola in 1492 and established a base in what is now the country of Haiti.

Suspect 2—Jean de Chat
Yuba City, California, is northeast of San Francisco.

Dances With Wolves won the Academy Award for Best Motion Picture in 1990.

Scorpions are arachnids, not insects, so Jean did not disobey his mother.

Scorpion stings are painful, but they rarely cause death.

Tropical cockroaches sometimes grow to five inches in length, and many are brightly colored.

Suspect 3—Perin Arnaud
Casablanca is on the coast of Morocco, Africa.

Irene Joliot-Curie died in 1956.

The finest caviar is sturgeon eggs, of which Russia, not Finland, is the world's leading producer. The eggs of whitefish, lumpfish and salmon, which are sometimes marketed as caviar, cost much less.

Truffles, a form of fungi, grow on or near the roots of oak trees. They are most often found three and a half inches below the ground.

Suspect 4—Bert "Mr. Beef" Baker
Whitefish, Montana, is southwest of Waterton Glacier International Peace Park, which is sometimes called Glacier National Park.

Clarence Birdseye died in 1956.

Typhoid fever, an infection caused by the Salmonella typhi bacteria, is spread through contaminated food.

There are more than 3,500 species of cockroaches.

Cockroaches don't live in refrigerators. They require a temperature exceeding 65 degrees Fahrenheit.

The Mystery of the Sabotaged Salad

The Mystery of the Toppled Treehouse

The Crime

Harrison Harrington, III, doted on his daughter. When she wanted a Cabbage Patch doll, he bought her fourteen Cabbage Patch dolls. When she wanted to go to Disney World, he chartered a plane and took her there. When she wanted a treehouse, he had a treehouse built for her on the grounds of the New England estate where she lived with her mother.

But, her treehouse was no ordinary plywood platform with a rope ladder. Angela Marie's treehouse was a replica of Windsor Castle, set high in the limbs of a towering oak. At her request, it was painted a florid pink, with a picture of Princess Barbie on one side and Prince Ken on the other.

Angela Marie spent many happy hours in her leaf-shaded aerie. But, one day, returning from a weekend with her father, she discovered that the oak had fallen under the relentless persuasion of a chain saw. All that remained of Windsor Castle was splintered pink debris.

The Problem

Who destroyed Angela Marie's treehouse?

The Suspects

Suspect 1: Bud Popkin

Bud Popkin, the gardener's son, was born in Gary, Indiana, near the shores of Lake Michigan, the year *The Last Emperor* won the Academy Award for Best Motion Picture.

"Angela Marie acted so sweet when grown-ups were watching," Bud Popkin informed us. "But she was spoiled, and she was mean. My father let me plant one of the Harrington's gardens with peonies because the peony is the state flower of the state where I was born. Angela Marie ran her bicycle through the garden and ruined it. She said she lost control when she ran over the garden hose I was using to water the flowers. Her mother got all hysterical about it and practically accused me of trying to murder her precious princess."

"But, lately all Angela Marie talked about was her castle. 'Your daddy can't afford to build you something like this, can he, Bud? He's only a gardener. Maybe if you're nice to me, I'll let you plant a garden around my treehouse.' 'I'd be happy to,' I told her. 'How would you like a garden of Rafflesia, the flower with the largest bloom in the world?' The little twit liked that idea. I didn't tell her that the Rafflesia is better known as the parasitic stinking corpse lily. I hated Angela Marie," Bud Popkin admitted candidly. "I'm glad her treehouse was sawed down. Too bad she wasn't in it at the time."

Bud Popkin's alibi: "I was in my room all weekend. My father caught me using some of his power tools and he grounded me."

Suspect 2: Jessica Tweeter

Jessica Tweeter, a neighbor, was born in Portage la Prairie, west of Winnipeg, Manitoba, Canada, the year Federico Fellini made *Juliet of the Spirits.*

Jessica is an avian aficionado with a particular fondness for owls. "Owls are closely related to hawks and eagles and other raptorial birds," Jessica Tweeter explained as she showed us around her expansive yard. "Although they can see perfectly well in the daytime, they prefer to hunt at night because that's when they catch moths and lightning bugs, which are the mainstay of their diets. My favorite owls are the burrowing owls. I have a whole colony of them roosting in the tops of my trees. I like to watch them from my second-floor balcony."

"Unfortunately, that wretched little Harrington girl could see them from her treehouse. She used to sit up there and throw rocks at them. Knowing the way her father spoils her rotten, they were probably imported rocks."

Jessica Tweeter's alibi: "I spent the weekend rebuilding a burrowing owl nest that Angela Marie had knocked out of a palmetto tree with a piece of gneiss. It's useless to try to talk to that child's parents about her destruction. Her father thinks she's perfect, and her mother would accuse my owls of spreading diseases."

Suspect 3: Penelope Harrington

Penelope Harrington, Angela Marie's mother, was born in Antofagasta, Chile, near the Tropic of Capricorn, the year Marilyn Monroe died.

"I have no idea what my ex-husband thought he was doing when he built Angela Marie that horrible death trap," Penelope Harrington complained. "I was terrified that she was going to plummet off one of the towers and maim herself for life. When I was a child, a friend of mine received a comminuted fracture of her humerus. The bone just splintered into pieces, and when it healed her arm was crooked. And, my cousin, Jason, ruptured his spleen when he fell out of his bedroom window. He had to have a splenectomy. I cringe whenever I think about it. What would Angela Marie do without a spleen? How would her body filter out the foreign organisms and old red blood cells from her blood stream? How would she store the bile needed to digest fat? Not that I allow her to eat fatty foods. I'm very careful about Angela Marie's diet. But, my husband..." Penelope Harrington let out a disapproving sigh.

"So many awful things can happen to a child. I prefer to keep Angela Marie inside the house where she'll be safe."

Penelope Harrington's alibi: "I was at the beauty shop all day. When I came home, I was so tired I went straight to my bedroom to rest. I didn't notice the condition of the treehouse until I heard Angela Marie screaming. Thank God she was all right. I was certain she had hurt herself."

Suspect 4: Jerome Wesley Spencer

Jerome Wesley Spencer, a professor of English history, was born in Swansea, Wales, near the Bristol Channel, the same year Charles, Prince of Wales was born.

"The original Windsor Castle, as you most probably know, is the chief residence of the rulers of Great Britain," Jerome Spencer informed us pedantically. "William the Conqueror chose the site, and Edward III started construction of the present structure. The chapel vault holds the bodies of Henry VIII, Charles I, William IV, George V, George VI, and Edward VII. The most important feature of the castle is the round keep, which Harrison Harrington replicated in the wrong proportions.

"The keep, the other four towers, the lower ward—they were all positioned inaccurately. And, then to paint it pink!" Jerome Spencer threw up his hands in a gesture of exasperation. "It was an abomination, and an insult to anglophiles everywhere."

Jerome Wesley Spencer's alibi: "I was at home perusing Sir William Blackstone's famous *Commentaries on the Laws of England.*"

The Solution

Jessica Tweeter didn't know much about owls (she probably had barn owls, not burrowing owls, nesting in her trees), but she loved them. She didn't want to see them hurt or driven away by a spoiled brat with rocks. Because Angela Marie's parents obviously didn't exert enough control over her to make her stop stoning owls, Jessica Tweeter got out her chain saw and removed the child's rock-throwing platform. She was careful to cut the tree so it wouldn't fall on any owl nests.

Information about the suspects

Suspect 1—Bud Popkin

Gary, Indiana, is near Lake Michigan.

The Last Emperor won the Academy Award for Best Motion Picture in 1987.

The peony is the state flower of Indiana.

The Rafflesia, the flower with the largest bloom in the world, is also known as the parasitic stinking corpse lily.

Suspect 2—Jessica Tweeter

Portage la Prairie is west of Winnipeg, Manitoba, Canada.

Federico Fellini made *Juliet of the Spirits* in 1965.

Owls are more closely related to night hawks and whippoorwills than they are to hawks and eagles.

Some, but not all, owls can see as well in the daytime as at night.

Owls are nocturnal hunters.

Owls will eat insects, but they prefer mice and other small mammals.

Burrowing owls do not nest in trees. They live in burrows in the ground, usually near colonies of prairie dogs, on which they prey.

The palmetto tree is a subtropical tree found in the southeastern United Sates, not in New England.

Suspect 3—Penelope Harrington

Antofagasta, Chile, is near the Tropic of Capricorn.

Marilyn Monroe died in 1962.

A comminuted fracture is one in which the bone splinters into pieces.

The humerus is the bone in the upper arm.

A splenectomy might be performed to remove a ruptured spleen.

The spleen filters out the foreign organisms and old red blood cells from the body's blood stream.

The gallbladder stores bile, which aids in the digestion of fats.

Suspect 4—Jerome Wesley Spencer

Swansea, Wales, is near the Bristol Channel.

Charles, Prince of Wales, was born in 1948.

The original Windsor Castle is the chief residence of the rulers of Great Britain. William the Conqueror chose the site, and Edward III started construction of the present structure.

The chapel vault holds the bodies of Henry VIII, Charles I, William IV, George V, George VI, and Edward VII.

Windsor Castle's most important feature is the round keep.

Sir William Blackstone wrote *Commentaries on the Laws of England.*

Difficult Mysteries

The Mystery of the Dead Director

The Crime

"You are a better swordsman than I am, Mr. Washington," Charles Cornwallis admitted wearily, tossing his sword to the floor in a gesture of defeat. "You are the victor. You and this new nation, and all your crazy notions of democracy for the common…" He got no further with his lines before the sound of a gunshot disturbed the filming of the made-for-TV movie *George Washington: First Blood.*

The cast and crew were confused by the unexpected intrusion. "There's no gun-shot in the script," the actor playing Cornwallis insisted angrily. "Darn it! That was the best performance I ever gave, and now we'll have to reshoot the entire sequence. Frank!" He screamed for the director.

But, Franklin Watterby didn't answer. The director was dead.

The Problem

Who killed Frank Watterby?

The Suspects

Suspect 1: Sidney Van Cleet

Sidney Van Cleet, a historian and author, was born in Cleethorpes, England, on the coast of the North Sea, the year *The Best Years of Our Lives* won the Academy Award for Best Motion Picture.

Sidney Van Cleet wrote the book on which the script for *George Washington: First Blood* was based. "Don't blame me for what Franklin Watterby did to this film," Van Cleet insisted vehemently. "It was a web of distortions and prevarications, a complete travesty of American history, disguised as a documentary about the American Revolution."

"It was bad enough when Franklin depicted George Washington as an impoverished young man walking twenty miles to attend classes at the University of Virginia Law School. But, when Franklin decided to shoot scenes of George Washington meeting with the spy Mata Hari, I threatened to expose him to *People* magazine. Franklin said to go ahead and cry to the media. That kind of publicity would double the audience for his film."

"I own a gun," Sidney Van Cleet admitted. "It's a harquebus, an early form of firearm that was used in the 1400s."

Sidney Van Cleet's alibi: "I was in my dressing room rereading one of my earlier books, *Murder Through the Ages.*"

Suspect 2: Dawn Ferrari

Dawn Ferrari, an ingenue, was born in Brindisi, on the heel of Italy's boot, the year James Riddle Hoffa disappeared.

Dawn Rerrari was cast in the role of Mrs. Washington, the first first lady of the United States. "Her name was Martha," Dawn said in a mellifluous Italian accent. "But, George Washington used to call her by her nickname, Patsy. She traveled with him to Valley Forge and Morristown, and when she wasn't with him, he wrote to her. He must have written very sensual letters because she burned them all before she died."

"I had some disagreements with the director," Dawn admitted frankly. "He wanted me to stumble through a swamp, vainly trying to reach New York City to stop Nathan Hale from being hanged. But, I refused to slog around in all that mud because it would have ruined my makeup. He didn't mean all those awful things he said about replacing me with another actress. He was angry at the time, but he got over his little snit. He even sent me a lovely gift to prove that all was forgiven."

"I own a handgun," Dawn Ferrari admitted. "It is a Colt .45 automatic pistol. I believe it was made in Hartford, Connecticut, in the factory Samuel Colt built to manufacture the guns used in the Mexican and Civil Wars. I realize that a handgun seems like a strange gift for a man to give a woman, but Franklin was worried about my safety. This is America, after all."

Dawn Ferrari's alibi: "I was in my dressing room applying a fresh coat of makeup. I had a big scene coming up soon."

Suspect 3: Holly Dooley

Holly Dooley, the vice-president of the studio that was financing *George Washington: First Blood,* was born in Long Beach, south of Los Angeles, the year Lyndon Baines Johnson became president of the United States.

"I grew up in the movie industry," Holly Dooley told us. "My father worked on Cecil B. DeMille's movie *The Birth of a Nation* and I had a bit part in *Close Encounters of the Third Kind*, the Steven Spielberg film that won the Academy Award for best movie in 1980. *George Washington: First Blood* was my chance to prove myself as a vice-president of a movie studio.

"And Franklin Watterby was ruining my chance," she admitted grimly. "First, he hired that European birdbrain to play George Washington's wife. Then, he started changing the course of American history to suit his artistic whims. If this movie had been released, I would be the laughing stock of the motion picture industry—not to mention unemployed."

"I prefer bows and arrows to guns. In fact, I'm quite good at clout shooting, in which the standard target used for all forms of target archery is placed flat on the ground. Do I own a handgun?" Holly Dooley seemed a bit uncomfortable when we asked the question. "Yes, as a matter of fact, I do. Doesn't everyone?"

Holly Dooley's alibi: "I was in the editing room looking at the early rushes of *George Washington: First Blood.* They were so bad they made me cringe."

Suspect 4: Marvina Watterby

Marvina Watterby, the director's widow, was born in Slaughter Beach, Delaware, on the coast of Delaware Bay, the year Rachel Carson's book *Silent Spring* was published.

"Franklin was under a lot of pressure," Marvina Watterby informed us, dabbing her tears away with a black lace handkerchief. "That horrible Van Cleet man was always berating him about his lack of integrity, and Holly Dooley was no better. Still, that doesn't excuse his lunatic infatuation with that asinine little actress, Dawn."

"He denied it, of course, but I knew that he was giving her expensive gifts—a diamond brooch and a set of emerald earrings. Then, he gave that actress the ruby slippers that were worn by Frances Gumm in *The Wizard of Oz,* when she was seventeen. Thank God he came to his senses before he died. He told me that he had finally seen Miss Ferrari for the vain, egotistical twit she really was. We were planning a second honeymoon on the Riviera as soon as *George Washington: First Blood* was finished."

"No, I don't own a handgun." Marvina Watterby answered our question. "I don't believe that private citizens should own guns, no matter what the second amendment guarantees. Franklin and I argued about that all the time. It's ironic that he was the victim of a right he believed in, isn't it?"

Marvina Watterby's alibi: "I was on the set during the filming of Cornwallis' surrender. I wasn't going to let Dawn Ferrari ever be alone with Franklin again."

The Solution

George Washington: First Blood, with all of its distortion of history, was becoming an embarrassment to the historian Sidney Van Cleet. But, it was Holly Dooley who had the most to lose when the movie was released. Her superiors at the movie studio would hold her responsible for financing this expensive turkey of a movie, and she would most likely be fired.

After seeing the rushes (which were so bad they made her cringe), she left the editing room with only one thought in her mind: Stop this movie from being finished. While everyone's attention was on the scene between George Washington and Charles Cornwallis, she pulled out her handgun and put an end to Franklin Watterby's distorted version of the American Revolution.

Information about the suspects

Suspect 1—Sidney Van Cleet
Cleethorpes, England, is on the coast of the North Sea.

The Best Years of Our Lives won the Academy Award for Best Motion Picture in 1946.

The harquebus was an early form of firearm that was used in the 1400s.

(See "Other Misinformation")

Suspect 2—Dawn Ferrari
Brindisi is on the heel of Italy's boot.

James Riddle Hoffa disappeared in 1975.

George Washington used to call his wife by her childhood nickname, Patsy.

Martha Washington traveled with George to Valley Forge and Morristown, New Jersey.

Before she died, Martha Washington burned all of the letters George had written to her.

Samuel Colt established a factory in Hartford, Connecticut, where he produced guns used in the Mexican and Civil Wars.

(See "Other Misinformation")

Suspect 3—Holly Dooley
Long Beach, California, is south of Los Angeles.

Lyndon Baines Johnson became president of the United States in 1963.

The Birth of a Nation was made by D.W. Griffith, not by Cecil B. DeMille.

Close Encounters of the Third Kind was a Steven Spielberg movie, but it was made in 1977 and did not win an Academy Award for best movie.

In clout shooting, the target is placed flat on the ground, but the clout target is about twelve times as large as the standard archery target.

Suspect 4—Marvina Watterby
Slaughter Beach, Delaware, is on the coast of Delaware Bay.

Rachel Carson's book *Silent Spring* was published in 1962.

Frances Gumm (Judy Garland) wore ruby slippers in *The Wizard of Oz*. She was seventeen when the movie was made.

The second amendment to the Constitution of the United States states that, for the purpose of maintaining a well-regulated millitia, citizens of the U.S. have the right to keep and bear arms.

Other Misinformation

Franklin Watterby had filled the script of *George Washington: First Blood* with distortions and lies, just as Sidney Van Cleet claimed. Those lies include the following:

Charles Cornwallis and George Washington did not fight face to face. They had two armies between them. Although Cornwallis was supposed to hand over his sword to Washington in a ceremony of surrender after the British troops were defeated at Yorktown, he said he was sick and sent his second in command to offer it. Washington was so annoyed that he sent *his* second in command to accept it.

George Washington did not have an impoverished childhood; his family was financially secure. He did not walk twenty miles to attend law school. In fact, he did not go to school at all after the age of 15.

Mata Hari was born one hundred years after the American Revolution. She could not have met George Washington.

Martha Washington was 44 years old when the Revolutionary War began, and 50 when it ended. She was certainly not a young woman with an Italian accent.

The Mystery of the Gentle Gypsy

The Crime

"The portrait was painted by Henri Julien Rousseau," Leslie Keech said as he pointed to the empty space on the wall of his study where the painting used to hang. "That alone made it worth a million dollars, but there was another reason it was valuable to me. The girl in the painting reminded me of my wife. She had the same gentle sadness in her beautiful, dark eyes. But, you want to know about the theft, don't you?" He suddenly remembered the matter at hand.

"The painting was here last night when we were having drinks with our guest, Thornton Nortonberry, the man from whom I bought the painting several years ago. That was 11:30 P.M. and I discovered the painting missing at 9:30 this morning. None of us heard the thief pick the lock on the back door, then come through the hallway to my study. Nor did my gardener, who lives in the cottage right inside the front gate of the estate, notice anyone on the grounds last night. It's hard to believe that someone could have carried a 4' x 3', 65-pound painting out of the house, past the gardener's cottage, and through the locked front gate, but that's apparently what happened. I have insurance, but money can never replace my lovely little gypsy."

The Problem

Who stole the painting of the gentle gypsy?

The Suspects

Suspect 1: Leslie Keech

Leslie Keech, was born in Cambridge, which is west of Boston, Massachusetts, the year that Mary Cassatt died.

"I'm going to tell you the truth," he confided. "But, please don't tell my wife. I lost most of my fortune in the stock market last week. We may have to fire the servants, sell the mansion, and move to a much smaller house. I don't mind for myself, but Marya is descended from Boleslaw, the first king of Poland. As a countess, she was raised in fine houses, surrounded by beautiful works of art. She lost her family and her fortune during World War II, but no one can take away the gentility that made me fall in love with her the first moment that we met."

"I had intended to sell the painting to raise the money I need to keep this house. That's why I invited Thornton Nortonberry to the house. But, last night I realized that I couldn't bear to part with the portrait. Henri Rousseau was a genius. He was a customs official in Paris, with no professional art training, and yet he created works that strongly influenced the surrealism movement of the 1920s."

"I decided to steal the painting from myself. It was insured," he explained. "If I stole it, the insurance company would pay me a million dollars, and I would still have the painting of that gentle little gypsy hidden in my secret vault. But, I didn't get a chance to steal it. Someone else stole it first."

Leslie Keech's alibi: "I was in my room planning every detail of the theft, which I intended to carry out tonight."

Suspect 2: Marya Keech

Marya Keech, Leslie's wife, was born in Gdansk, which is sometimes called Danzig, on the northern coast of Poland, the year that Georgie O'Keeffe married Alfred Stieglitz.

"I am going to tell you the truth," Marya Keech confided. "But, I beg you not to tell my husband. That portrait was not painted by Rousseau. It was painted by a Polish artist who made his living forging works in other artists' styles. I know this to be true because I posed for it in exchange for a few coins with which to buy a loaf of bread."

"My husband is so proud to be married to Countess Marya Politchika, I have never had the courage to tell him that the real Marya Politchika died when Germany and the U.S.S.R. fought for control of Poland in 1941. I stole the purse I found beside her body," Mrs. Keech confessed. "Inside the purse I found a passport, money, a ticket to America, and a letter from a distant cousin Marya had never met."

"You have to understand how desperate life was in Poland during World War II. Much of Warsaw was destroyed. Six million Poles died, and half of them were Jews. I would have done anything to survive," Mrs. Keech admitted. "So, I came to the United States with Marya's passport, and I have lived as her for the past 40 years. Those desperately unhappy times were forgotten until Leslie bought that wretched painting. Now, I live in constant fear that he will guess the truth. How can he continue to love me if he finds out that I have lied to him about my true identity ever since we met?"

Marya Keech's alibi: "I was soaking in a warm tub, hoping to ease the osteoarthritis pains in my hands and neck. The doctor informs me that there is no cure. But, warm water and a few aspirin usually make me feel more comfortable."

Suspect 3: Thorton Nortonberry

Thorton Nortonberry, an art dealer, was born in Toledo, Spain, which is south of Madrid, the year that Edvard Munch died.

"I'm going to tell you the truth," Mr. Nortonberry confided. "But, my reputation would be ruined if you told Leslie Keech. That portrait wasn't painted by Rousseau. It was forged by a Polish artist who was an old friend of my father's. When I last saw him, the painter was a pathetic old man suffering from a form of lead poisoning called painter's colic. The painting he asked me to sell for him had the look of a Rousseau—the bold colors, the decorative patterns, and the highly polished surface of the canvas. I misrepresented the painting to Leslie Keech in order to earn the painter enough money to die in comfort."

"But, I am not skilled at fraud, so I panicked when Leslie Keech told me he wanted to sell the gypsy painting. Anybody who would spend a million dollars on a painting would bring along his own expert to look at it, and my lie would be discovered. There was nothing I could do but steal the painting before Leslie Keech had a chance to sell it."

"The most expensive painting ever stolen was the Mona Lisa. If someone could steal a painting like that from the Louvre, surely I could steal a forged Rousseau from a private home. But, I'm no better a thief than I am a liar," Thornton Nortonberry admitted. "When I got there I had a few drinks to work up my courage. I had a few more drinks with dinner, then a few more after that."

Thornton Nortonberry's alibi: "I don't remember anything after Mrs. Keech graciously showed me to the guest room. I must have passed out from all the alcohol I consumed."

Suspect 4: Bill McKenney

Bill McKenney, the Keech's gardener, was born in Van Buren, Maine, near the Maine-New Brunswick border, the year Cloris Leachman won the Academy Award for Best Supporting Actress in *The Last Picture Show.*

"I'm going to tell you the truth, since you're going to find out about it anyway when you run my name through the police computer," Bill McKenney said as he raked grass clippings into heavy plastic trash bags. "But, please don't tell Mr. and Mrs. Keech because they'd fire me if they knew. I've got a prison record. A judge sent me to Alcatraz for three years for breaking into houses and stealing stereo equipment. I was framed. The eighteen stereos they found in my apartment were all birthday presents fror my friends."

Bill McKenney's alibi: "I spent most of the evening putting in the new herb garden that Mrs. Keech has been wanting. I dug up twenty square feet of ground and mixed some dehydrated cow manure into the soil. You can see the new garden right over there; I've just finished planting coca shrubs and hemp. I stopped around 10 P.M. to have supper."

The Solution

Marya Keech had a reason to steal the painting, but it is unlikely that an elderly woman with osteoarthritis in her hands and neck would have the strength to lift a 65-pound painting down from the wall. Thornton Nortonberry might have stolen the painting, but he was too inebriated. Leslie Keech planned to steal the painting, but he was too late. Bill McKenney, however, had experience at breaking and entering, as well as the physical strength to carry the painting out of the house. The motive for the theft was money, but Bill McKenney was due for a shock. Because it wasn't painted by Rousseau, the painting wasn't valuable enough to steal.

Bill McKenney waited until all the lights were out in the Keech household. Then, he picked the back door lock and stole the painting of the gypsy. Unable to sneak it off the estate that night, he wrapped it in plastic garbage bags and buried it in the new herb bed, which was exactly one foot wider and longer than the painting.

Information about the suspects

Suspect 1—Leslie Keech
Cambridge is west of Boston, Massachusetts.

Mary Cassatt died in 1926.

Boleslaw became the first king of Poland in 1025.

Henri Rousseau was a minor customs official in Paris until he retired to paint.

Rousseau had no professional art training.

Rousseau's work strongly influenced the surrealism movement of the 1920s.

Suspect 2—Marya Keech
Gdansk, which is sometimes referred to on maps as Danzig, is on the northern coast of Poland.

Georgia O'Keeffe married Alfred Stieglitz in 1924.

Both Germany and the U.S.S.R. invaded Poland in 1939. In 1941, Germany attacked the U.S.S.R. and seized control of all of Poland.

Much of Warsaw was destroyed during World War II. Six million Poles (half of them Jews) died during the war.

Osteoarthritis has no cure.

Aspirin is the most commonly used drug for osteoarthritis.

Suspect 3—Thornton Nortonberry
Toledo, Spain, is south of Madrid.

Edvard Munch died in 1944.

Painter's colic is a form of lead poisoning.

Henri Rousseau is known for his bold colors, decorative patterns, and the highly polished surface of his canvases.

The most expensive painting ever stolen was the Mona Lisa, stolen from the Louvre in Paris in 1911.

Suspect 4—Bill McKenney
Van Buren, Maine is near the Maine-New Brunswick border.

Cloris Leachman won the Academy Award in 1971 for Best Supporting Actress in *The Last Picture Show.*

Alcatraz, the federal prison in San Francisco Bay, was closed in 1963, eight years before Bill McKenney was born.

One of the ways to create twenty square feet of garden space is to dig a garden that is five feet long and four feet wide. The missing painting measured four feet by three feet.

The coca shrub produces cocaine. Hemp produces marijuana. It is unlikely that Mrs. Keech would want either of them planted in her herb bed.

The Mystery of the Glowing Ghost

The Crime

The trouble started six months ago. A group of guests met in the parlor of the run-down Seaside Hotel to hold a séance, but the spirit the group succeeded in raising from the dead refused to go away. "It's my brother Boris," explained Beatrice Bozelman, the owner of the hotel. "He was a rude, obnoxious freeloader when he was alive, and I'm sorry to say that death has not changed him one iota."

Boris Bozelman had choked to death on a meatball sandwich in one of the guest rooms of his sister's hotel. The afternoon prior to his death, Boris Bozelman had told everyone in the hotel that he had a great deal of money in his room, but no money was found after his death. His sister claims he never had any money. That was just a boast to impress his daughter Bunny, who was still young enough to adore her blustering popinjay of a father.

Now, the ghost of Boris Bozelman roams the halls of the Seaside Hotel late at night, telling insulting jokes and smoking an odious cigar, which he sometimes leaves smoldering on the furniture. A dozen people have seen him glowing in the dark as he stomps up and down the stairs.

Since his arrival, guests have checked out of the hotel, leaving most of the guest rooms empty. Beatrice Bozelman cannot pay the bills and may have to sell the hotel.

The Problem

Who is the ghost of Boris Bozelman?

The Suspects

Suspect 1: Madame B. Yonde

Madame B. Yonde, is a spiritualist and medium. Beverly Yonde was born in Komadi, Hungary, near the Romanian border, the year Noel Coward wrote *Blithe Spirit.*

"My countryman, Ehrich Weiss, didn't believe in spiritualists," Madame B. Yonde confided. "He spent a great deal of time debunking séances after he made a name for himself as an escape artist. But, many influential people have been interested in the occult. The Magi who visited the Christ child were astrologers and interpreters of dreams."

"I conduct séances from time to time. Sometimes George Washington appears and says a few words. But, I've never had a ghost stay the way Boris Bozelman's ghost is staying. I've never conjured such a rude ghost, either. A few nights ago, I woke to find his spirit glowing in the corner of my bedroom. When I demanded to know what he was doing there, he had the audacity to tell me that I snore loudly enough to wake the dead! Then, he said that he was looking for his money, and he doesn't intend to leave until he's found it."

Madame B. Yonde's alibi: "I did it! I'm responsible. I brought that horrible ghost into this house. All I wanted to do was provide a little entertainment for the other guests. I didn't know how much trouble I'd be causing for poor Beatrice and her hotel by bringing the spirit of Boris Bozelman back from the other side."

Suspect 2: Bunny Bozelman

Bunny Bozelman, the daughter of the dearly departed Boris Bozelman, was born in Owatonna, Minnesota, south of St. Paul, the year Jean George won the Newbery Medal for *Julie of the Wolves.*

Bunny has lived with her aunt Beatrice ever since her father died. She was ten years old at the time, and her relationship with her aunt has not always been smooth. She thinks Beatrice Bozelman is too strict and far too stingy with money. She also thinks her aunt found her father's money and kept it for herself. Beatrice thinks that Bunny is selfish and lazy and boastful, just like Bunny's father."

Bunny's dream is to start a company to manufacture and sell cosmetics. "I've been experimenting with cosmetics made from aloe, which is a plant that grows profusely in northern forests although it is related to the cactus. I'd like to combine aloe oil with nectar of the *Puya raimondii,* a fragrant South African plant. The problem is, the *Puya raimondii* is the slowest flowering plant in the world. It takes close to 50 years for a plant to mature enough to flower, and after that it blooms only once every five years, so developing my special line of Bunny Bozelman's *Puya raimondii* and aloe cosmetics would take time, and a lot of money. I tried to get some money from Aunt Beatrice," she said bitterly, "but she's so tight she squeaks. The least she could do is give me back the money she took from my father's room after he died."

Bunny Bozelman's alibi: "Sure I was in the hotel every time someone saw my father's ghost. It's me he's trying to contact. He's trying to tell me where to find the money so I can start my business. I don't blame the guests for checking out. If I had enough money I'd get out of this dump, too. I think Aunt Beatrice should sell it to Mr. Dodger, the real estate agent, and I've told her that at least a hundred times."

Suspect 3: Vernon Pimplus

Vernon Pimplus, a chemist, was born in Hermosillo, Mexico, not far from the Gulf of California, the year Lars Onsager won the Nobel Prize for Chemistry.

Vernon works for the Wod Chemical Company, experimenting with bioluminescent compounds. "Sure, it looks pretty, but bioluminescence can be used for treachery and deceit," Vernon told us. "Fireflies use cold light signals to attract mates, but the females of some species of fireflies imitate the signals of other species to lure the males to them. Then they kill and eat them!" Vernon shuddered. "Lanternfish use their photophores to attract prey. Even sardines are betrayed by luminescent organisms in the sea."

"It's a creepy area of research. Thank the stars I have Bunny to talk to," Vernon added shyly. "She always wants to hear about my work, and sometimes she stops by the lab to see me."

Vernon Pimplus' alibi: "The night of the séance I hid under a table when Boris Bozelman appeared, so I didn't get a look at him. Whenever I hear him in the hallway, I pull the blankets over my head and close my eyes. I've never seen the ghost, but I know it's real. Bunny has told me all about it."

Suspect 4: Roger Dodger

Roger Dodger, a real estate agent, was born in Sari, Iran, near the Caspian Sea, the year Frank Lloyd Wright died.

Roger thinks that the Seaside Hotel should be torn down. "Old hotels like this are a thing of the past," he told us. "If this place were mine, I'd tear it down and get a good architect in here to design a high-rise condominium project. I'd hire Ludwig Mies van der Rohe, whose philosophy is 'more is better.' Or maybe Louis Isadore Kahn, who was born in my hometown in Iran. He had a theory about "served" and "servant" spaces in buildings. He liked to highlight the "served" spaces where people live and work, and hide the "servant" spaces, like stairwells and air ducts. Wasted space is wasted money, know what I mean? Yes, sir, I'd put up a nice concrete and glass tower and charge the tenants a small fortune for the privilege of living there. I keep offering to buy the place from Mrs. Bozelman, but she's the stubborn type. She's going to keep this place open until there isn't a guest left. But, the way things are going now, that won't be much longer."

Roger Dodger's alibi: "Hey, I won't pretend I'm sorry this is going on. I want to buy this piece of property so badly I'd be willing to pay someone to run Beatrice Bozelman off. But, I wasn't here the night of the séance. I was taking a walk on the beach all by myself. And, all the other nights the ghost appeared—I was walking on the beach those nights, too."

The Solution

Roger Dodger was willing to pay someone to run Beatrice Bozelman off, and Bunny was happy to take his money. Together they faked the ghost of Boris Bozelman, hoping that the apparition would drive guests away and force Beatrice to sell the Seaside Hotel.

Bunny knew how to make cosmetics. All she needed was a compound that would glow in the dark, and she obtained that the day she visited the love-struck Vernon Pimplus at his laboratory. She made up Roger Dodger to look like her father's ghost. (He lied when he said he wasn't around during Boris Bozelman's appearances. He was very much around.) Vernon Pimplus might have been able to figure out what was going on, but he never took the blankets off his head long enough to look at the faked ghost of Boris Bozelman.

Boris Bozelman's choking death and his missing money are red herrings; they have nothing at all to do with the plot to force Beatrice Bozelman out of her hotel, except, perhaps, to give Bunny Bozelman the extra motive of revenge. Boris Bozelman probably didn't have a cent to his name the day he tried to swallow far too many meatballs.

Information about the suspects

Suspect 1—Madame B. Yonde
Komadi, Hungary, is near the Romanian border.

Noel Coward wrote *Blithe Spirit* in 1941.

Ehrich Weiss, who was better known as Harry Houdini, was born in Hungary.

Houdini spent a great deal of time debunking séances after he made a name for himself as an escape artist.

The Magi were astrologers and interpreters of dreams.

Suspect 2—Bunny Bozelman
Owatonna, Minnesota, is south of St. Paul.

Jean George won the Newbery Medal for *Julie of the Wolves* in 1973.

Aloe grows in South Africa and other warm climates.

Aloe is related to lilies, not cactus.

Puya raimondii is a Bolivian, not a South African, plant.

The *Puya raimondii* is the slowest flowering plant in the world. One cultivated plant bloomed after 28 years, but in its natural habitat it takes 80–150 years to bloom. Then it dies.

Suspect 3—Vernon Pimplus
Hermosillo, Mexico, is not far from the Gulf of California.

Lars Onsager won the Nobel Prize for Chemistry in 1968.

Fireflies give off a bioluminescent glow called cold light.

The females of some species of fireflies imitate the signals of other species to lure the males to them. Then they kill and eat them.

Lanternfish use their photophores to attract prey.

Fishermen sometimes locate sardines by noting the glow of tiny organisms that have been disturbed by the sardines' movements.

Suspect 4—Roger Dodger
Sari, Iran, is near the Caspian Sea.

Frank Lloyd Wright died in 1959.

Ludwig Mies van de Rohe's philosophy was "less is more," not "more is better." He died in 1969.

Louis Isadore Kahn was born in Estonia, not Iran.

Kahn considered "servant" spaces, like stairwells and air ducts, essential to a building's beauty and incorporated them into his designs.

The Mystery of Jolly Mama's Missing Muffins

The Crime

The Puff-Up Bakery makes bread, cookies, and pretzel sticks, but its most successful product is Jolly Mama's Tutti-Frutti Breakfast Muffins. John Hockingham, the president of Puff-Up Bakery, bought the recipe five years ago and spent $2 million on advertising to make it the best-selling breakfast muffin in the country. But, now there's trouble in the world of breakfast muffins. Health-Nut, a rival bakery, has put out a Frutti-Tutti breakfast muffin that is almost identical to Jolly Mama's Tutti-Frutti muffins, except that the Health-Nut muffins do not contain food additives. People are switching to Health-Nut's Frutti-Tutti muffins, and John Hockingham is livid.

"They've got my recipe!" he told us. "And, I know exactly how it happened. I accidentally left my safe unlocked the day I went on a business trip to Oklahoma City. Someone in my company must have copied the recipe and sold it to the Health-Nut Bakery. You find that low-life, two-faced slime for me, and I'll make sure that person never works for any bakery again!"

The Problem

Who gave the Jolly Mama recipe to Health-Nut?

The Suspects

Suspect 1: Harriet Hockingham

Harriet Hockingham, the wife of the president of Puff-Up Bakery, was born in Hollywood, Florida, north of Miami, the year that *The Bronze Bow* by Elizabeth George Speare won the Newbery Medal.

Harriet is bored with her life. "Cleaning and cooking and cleaning some more. How would you like it?" Harriet complained. "Do you think I care if the kitchen floor smells like lemons? No! I want to start a plumbing business."

"I know all about plumbing," Harriet Hockingham insisted. "The word 'plumbing' comes from the Latin word 'plumbum,' which means lead. The ancient Romans, who used lead pipes in their plumbing systems, had faucets and a sewerage system that carried their wastes to the rivers. A type of flush toilet was invented in the 1500s, and in the 1860s, Sir Thomas Crapper improved the toilet. See, I know everything I need to know to apply for a plumber's license, but my cheapskate husband won't give me the money I need to start my own company. He wants me to stay home 'where a woman belongs.'"

Harriet Hockingham's alibi: "It never occurred to me to steal the recipe for Jolly Mama's muffins. I wish I had. At any rate, I was at home that day, deodorizing my bathtub."

Suspect 2: Robert MacIntosh

Robert MacIntosh, the chemist for Puff-Up Bakery, was born in Mexico, Maine, just north of Rumford, the year Linus Carl Pauling won the Nobel Prize for Chemistry.

Robert MacIntosh credits himself with improving the Jolly Mama muffin recipe.

"When it was brought to me, it was just flour and eggs and sugar and chopped-up bits of fruit," he informed us. "I developed the balance of food additives it needed. Sequestrants, like ethylenediamine tetra-acetate and citric acid, keep trace minerals in the food from reacting with oxygen. Preservatives, like benzoic acid, sorbic acid, and sulfur dioxide, stop the growth of microorganisms. Humectants, like glycerol and sorbitol, keep the muffins moist. Emulsifiers and stabilizers, like algin, carrageenin, and pectin, hold the elements of the muffin together. Monosodium glutamate enhances the flavors of the food, and antioxidants, like butylated hydroxyanisol, propyl gallate, and ascorbic acid, prevent the compounds in food from combining with oxygen."

"Now those muffins can sit on supermarket shelves for six months without going stale. But, did I get a bonus for my work? NO! John Hockingham shook my hand and said, 'Well done, old chap.' He's like that—cheap."

Robert MacIntosh's alibi: "I was in my laboratory feeding Puff-Up Oven-Ready Pancakes to my mice."

Suspect 3: Lila Laverne

Lila Laverne, John Hockingham's secretary, was born in Bon Air, Virginia, near Richmond, the year Steven Spielberg directed *Jaws*.

Lila can't type, can't take dictation, won't make coffee, and hates being a secretary. "But a girl's got to eat, y'know," Lila told us as she filed her crimson fingernails. "Actually, what I really want to be is an actress, but I need acting lessons and an agent and a decent wardrobe to wear to casting calls.

That kind of money isn't easy to save on the salary Mr. Hockingham pays me. That man's so stingy, he makes Ebenezer Scrooge look like Santa Claus."

Lila Laverne's alibi: "Since Mr. Hockingham wasn't around that day, I snuck out to the Community Theater to try out for a role in this great new play called *Coriolanus.* It was written by some English guy. I don't remember his name, but the other actresses were gossiping about him. Like, he was the mayor's son in a small English town, and he got married to a woman who was eight years older than he was, and then he took off for London. Then—here's the weird part—no one knows what he did for seven years, and he's certainly not telling. But, the other actresses said his stuff was great and you get to wear great costumes. So, what do I care what he did when he was incommunicado?"

Suspect 4: Mrs. Hildegard Wintergarten

Mrs. Hildegard Wintergarten, alias Jolly Mama, was born in Eufala, Alabama, near the Alabama-Georgia border, the year that Frank B. Kellogg won the Nobel prize for Peace.

Five years ago, Mrs. Wintergarten sold her recipe for Tutti-Frutti Breakfast Muffins to the Puff-Up Bakery for $2,000. "Mr. Hock-ingham has made millions with that recipe," she told us. "And, all I got was a miserable $2,000. But, that's not why I'm furious. Those Tutti-Frutti muffins were healthful and nutritious. My recipe calls for bread flour, which has three times the protein found in cake flour. Since every person in the United States consumes an average of 75 pounds of flour a year, I think the protein content makes a difference."

"And, they added chemicals—sixteen of them!" she cried, pointing to the label on the Jolly Mama package. "I don't care what that hideous little chemist says about some food additives being natural. Strychnine is a natural by-product of the baobab tree, but I certainly wouldn't want it in my food! I'll tell you the truth," Mrs. Wintergarten confided, "I'm glad the recipe was stolen. The Health-Nut version of my muffins is far superior to Puff-Up's version."

Mrs. Hildegard Wintergarten's alibi: "I was here in my kitchen perfecting the recipe for my giant granola jumble cookies. When I get them right, I'm going to sell the recipe to Health-Nut because they have assured me that they will never add chemicals to anything they bake."

The Mystery of Jolly Mama's Missing Muffins

The Solution

Jolly Mama didn't like the long list of food additives with which the Puff-Up Bakery had "improved" her muffins, so she sold her recipe again, this time to the Health-Nut Bakery. Because she created the recipe in the first place, she didn't have to break into John Hockingham's office to steal it.

Information about the suspects

Suspect 1—Harriet Hockingham

Hollywood, Florida, is north of Miami.

The Bronze Bow by Elizabeth George Speare won the Newbery Medal in 1962.

The word "plumbing" comes from the Latin word "*plumbum*," which means lead.

The ancient Romans, who used lead pipes in their plumbing systems, had faucets and a sewerage system that carried their wastes to the rivers.

A type of flush toilet was invented in the 1500s.

Sir Thomas Crapper improved the flush toilet in the 1860s.

Suspect 2—Robert MacIntosh

Mexico, Maine, is just north of Rumford.

Linus Carl Pauling won the Nobel Prize for Chemistry in 1954.

Sequestrants, like ethylenediamine tetra-acetate (EDTA) and citric acid, keep trace minerals in the food from reacting with oxygen.

Preservatives, like benzoic acid, sorbic acid, and sulfur dioxide, stop the growth of microorganisms.

Humectants, like glycerol and sorbitol, keep food moist.

Emulsifiers and stabilizers, like algin, carrageenin, and pectin, hold the elements of food together.

Monosodium glutamate enhances the flavors of the food.

Antioxidants, like butylated hydroxyanisol (BHA), propyl gallate, and ascorbic acid, prevent the compounds in food from combining with oxygen.

Suspect 3—Lila Laverne

Bon Air, Virginia, is near Richmond.

Steven Spielberg directed *Jaws* in 1975.

Coriolanus was written by the English dramatist William Shakespeare.

Shakespeare was the son of the mayor of Stratford-upon-Avon.

He married a woman eight years his elder.

No one knows what Shakespeare did between 1585 and 1592.

Suspect 4—Mrs. Hildegard Wintergarten

Eufala, Alabama, is near the Alabama-Georgia border.

Frank B. Kellogg won the Nobel Prize for Peace in 1929.

Bread flour contains at least 11 percent protein. Cake flour contains less than $8\frac{1}{2}$ percent protein. Bread flour contains more protein, but not three times as much.

Every person in the United States consumes an average of 120 pounds of flour a year.

Strychnine comes from the *nux vomica* tree, not the baobab tree.

The Mystery of the Missing Mummy Jars

The Crime

It wasn't easy for Amir-del-Shabib and Professor Delbert Demsley to make the arrangements that brought the Egyptian Tut-Tut-Tut Exhibit to Boston. Egyptian officials wanted Professor Demsley's museum to hire extra security guards to protect the exhibit 24 hours a day. They also wanted 75 percent of all profits made from postcard and T-shirt sales.

After several years of wrangling, Shabib and Demsley worked out a compromise with the Egyptian government. Egypt would receive 50 percent of the profit from postcard and T-shirt sales; Professor Demsley's museum would pay the cost of an electronic alarm system; and Amir-del-Shabib himself would travel with the exhibit to install and monitor the security devices.

Unfortunately, Amir-del-Shabib's presence in Boston did not prevent an embarrassing and mystifying theft. Four gold canopic jars were stolen from the exhibit. They were found in the alley behind the museum a few hours after the theft was reported, but their contents were gone.

The Problem

Who stole the canopic jars?

The Suspects

Suspect 1: Amir-del-Shabib

Amir-del-Shabib, the Cairo Museum official who was traveling with the Tut-Tut-Tut Exhibit, was born in El Minya, which is sometimes spelled Al Minya, Egypt, on the banks of the Nile River, the year Howard Carter died.

"I like America," he told us. "I attended Yale University here in Boston twenty years ago. As a matter of fact, Professor Demsley and I were roommates. That is why I worked so hard to bring this exhibit to Boston. But, this theft…" He shrugged his shoulders despondently, "This will make furture exhibits even more difficult to arrange."

"I don't blame your country for this theft," he continued philosophically. "Even in my own country there are thieves. Three years ago, someone broke into the Cairo Museum and purloined four priceless amulets once worn by Tutankhamen's beautiful wife Nefertiti. Even though every museum and art dealer in Egypt was alerted, those exquisite artifacts were never recovered.

"Thank God the canopic jars were returned," Amir said. "The inscriptions on them tell us much about life in 937 B.C. when Tutankhamen became king."

Amir-del-Shabib's alibi: "At the time of the theft, I was dining with my old friend Professor Demsley. We were discussing our mediocre salaries over baked stuffed lobster and fine cognac."

Suspect 2: Professor Delbert Demsley

Professor Delbert Demsley, the curator of the museum, was born in Punxsutawney, Pennsylvania, northwest of Altoona, the year Franklin Delano Roosevelt died. The professor was Amir-del-Shabib's roommate in college.

"Those were the days," Professor Demsley sighed. "Amir and I were going to set the world on fire. Fame, fortune, beautiful women, fine houses—we were going to have them all. But, you want to hear about the theft," he said recalling himself from his nostalgic thoughts.

"It's a bizarre piece of larceny. The night watchman at the museum called me at 9:30 P.M. to tell me that the canopic jars were missing. By the time Amir and I arrived at the museum, they had been found in the alley, but they had been emptied of their contents. I can't imagine who would want the contents of those canopic jars. The unguents and oils might have been valuable back in 417 A.D., when King Tut and his wife, Cleopatra, were alive, but they would be dried up and useless now."

Professor Delbert Demsley's alibi: "I was in my apartment having dinner with Amir. We were just about to watch a videotape of *Raiders of the Lost Ark* when the night watchman phoned me."

Suspect 3: Harry Halloway

Harry Halloway, the night watchman at the museum, was born in Crete, Nebraska, southwest of Lincoln, the year *From Here to Eternity* won the Academy Award for Best Motion Picture.

"I have a confession to make," Harry told us sheepishly. "But, I'd appreciate it if you didn't pass the information on to Professor Demsley because he'd have me fired for sure if he found out. I discovered those jars missing about 9:00, but I didn't call the

Professor until 9:30 because I needed time to get a friend of mine out of here."

Harry's friend was a winsome blonde named Rhoda, whose avocation is astrology. "She's really into this Tut thing," Harry explained. "She saw that Boris Karloff movie *The Mummy* 35 times and when she found out I worked at the museum, she asked if she could come in and look around. I couldn't see any harm in it. Besides, it gets pretty lonely here at night."

"It's especially lonely around that Tut Exhibit," Harry confided in a whisper. "It gives me the crawling creeps to even think about it. You know what they used to do when they made a mummy? They used to pull the brains out through the poor guy's nose. And then they put the body in sodium carbonate, which is a kind of salt, until all of the tissues dried out like some kind of human beef jerky. Yecch!"

Harry Halloway's alibi: "I was on duty all night. Of course, with Rhoda here, I wasn't paying as much attention as I should have."

Suspect 4: Toni Littlefeather

Toni Littlefeather, Professor Demsley's assistant curator, was born in Deadwood, South Dakota, near the South Dakota-Wyoming border, one hundred years after Black Kettle was attacked by General George Armstrong Custer. She is a full-blooded Native American, a descendant of the Hunkpapa Sioux tribe for which Sitting Bull was a medicine man. "My people killed George Armstrong Custer," she admitted proudly.

Toni has very strong opinions about what should be in a museum and what should not be. "Human remains are not the same as a clay pot," she told us. "We would not put the embalmed body of President Millard Fillmore on display. Why, then, do we put King Tutankhamen's mummy on exhibit? Is it any different?"

"The deceased should be properly buried," she insisted vehemently. "It is indecent to put a person's body, or even pieces of the body, on display for people to gawk at."

Toni Littlefeather's alibi: "I was at home reading *The Last of the Mochicans* by James Fenimore Cooper."

The Solution

Amir-del-Shabib and Professor Delbert Demsley didn't pay attention during their history classes when they roomed together at Yale. Professor Demsley did not know what the canopic jars contained. Neither of them knew the name of Tutankhamen's wife or the year that Tutankhamen came to the throne of Egypt.

Obviously, the two old friends stole the canopic jars together. As curator, Professor Demsley would have had a key to the museum. Amir-del-Shabib was in charge of security for the exhibit, so he would have known how to avoid setting off the alarm. But, why would they have stolen mummy guts?

They didn't. Shabib had discarded them several years before when he was looking for a safe place to hide the amulets he had stolen from the Cairo Museum. Then, realizing that he couldn't sell the amulets in Egypt because all the museums and art dealers had been alerted to the theft, he involved Professor Demsley in his scheme to smuggle them into America in the canopic jars that were part of the Tut-Tut-Tut Exhibit.

Their motive was money. Both men had a taste for fine cognac and juicy lobster, for which they needed more than their mediocre salaries.

Information about the suspects

Suspect 1—Amir-del-Shabib
El Minya, or Al Minya, Egypt, is on the banks of the Nile River.

Howard Carter died in 1939.

Yale is in New Haven, Connecticut, not Boston, Massachusetts.

King Tutankhamen came to the throne of Egypt in 1347 B.C.

Tutankhamen's wife was Ankhesenpaaten (or Ankhesenamun), not Nefertiti.

Suspect 2—Professor Delbert Demsley
Punxsutawney, Pennsylvania, is northwest of Altoona.

Franklin Delano Roosevelt died in 1945.

Canopic jars contain the heart, liver, and other internal organs taken from the body during mummification, not oils and unguents.

King Tutankhamen came to the throne of Egypt in 1347 B.C.

Tutankhamen's wife was Ankhesenpaaten (or Ankhesenamun), not Cleopatra.

Suspect 3—Harry Halloway
Crete, Nebraska, is southwest of Lincoln, Nebraska.

From Here to Eternity won the Academy Award for best motion picture in 1953.

Boris Karloff starred in a movie titled *The Mummy.*

Brains were removed through the nose during mummification. They were thrown away because the Egyptians didn't think they were necessary in the afterlife.

In the Egyptian process of mummification, the body was placed in natron (sodium carbonate, which is a form of salt) in order to dry the tissues.

Suspect 4—Toni Littlefeather
Deadwood, South Dakota, is near the South Dakota-Wyoming border.

Black Kettle was attacked by General George Armstrong Custer in 1868. Toni Littlefeather was born one hundred years later in 1968.

Sitting Bull was medicine man to the Hunkpapa Sioux tribe that killed George Armstrong Custer.

Millard Fillmore was a president of the United States.

James Fenimore Cooper wrote *The Last of the Mohicans.*

The Mystery of the Obese Ornithologist

The Crime

For twenty years, Reginald Robbins spent Christmas Day exactly the same way: he and a small group of friends went bird-watching on the five hundred acres of land he owned in western Massachusetts. Everyone gathered at the ornithologist's house at 5 A.M. for coffee and a hearty breakfast. Then, they went outside, each taking a separate path through the woods or along the hills that overlooked the Connecticut River. Each person carried a pair of binoculars, a bird identification book (written by Reginald Robbins himself), and a notebook in which to write down every bird seen and the time of sighting. At noon, everyone returned to the house to eat Christmas dinner and compare their lists of birds.

But, this Christmas Day was different. When Lydia Robbins and Gregory Slimease arrived at the house (promptly at 5 A.M.), they were met at the door by Reginald Robbins' research assistant, Donald Dimpthwaite. He told them that he and Reginald had had an altercation, after which Reginald had stormed out of the house without his notebook (although he did remember his binoculars and bird identification

book). Reginald's young bride, Bambi Robbins, had asked Donald to wait for the other guests while she went after Reginald and tried to calm him down.

Lydia, Gregory, and Donald settled down to eat a hearty breakfast. Then, at 6:00 A.M., they set out together. Before they reached the woods (where they would all take separate paths), they met Bambi, who told them that Reginald had gotten over his "silly little tantrum." He had sighted a great many birds and had been so busy watching them through his binoculars that he had asked her to jot down the names and times on a piece of paper he had found inside his bird identification book.

Finally, realizing that she was cold, Reginald had kissed her on the cheek and told her to return to the house. Reginald had promised to return at noon and play the genial host, even to Donald Dimpthwaite.

Alas, Reginald did not return. At 1:30 P.M. a search party made up of Bambi, Donald, Lydia, Gregory, and the Robbins' cook found him at the base of a granite cliff. He had apparently fallen sometime earlier that day, and he was now as dead as a dodo. His copy of the bird identification guide lay

beside him, and in it was a folded piece of
paper that looked like this:

bobolink	*5:15*
Baltimore oriole	*5:20*
catbird	*5:35*
indigo bunting	*5:50*
nighthawk	*6:10*

Bambi's handwriting

Fold in paper

pick up Christmas cards
1 pint rocky road ice cream

bluejay	*6:37*
starling	*6:54*

Reginald's handwriting

The Problem

Who killed Reginald Robbins?

The Suspects

Suspect 1: Bambi Robbins

Bambi Robbins, Reginald Robbins' wife, was born in Paradise Valley, in the southeast corner of Nevada, the year that Betsy Byars won the Newbery Medal for *Summer of the Swans.* She was a waitress in an all-night doughnut shop when she met Reginald. They were married six months later.

"Reggie wasn't like any of the other men I'd dated," Bambi told us. "He was so sweet and considerate. The day after his divorce from Lydia was final, we were married. We spent a two-week honeymoon on the Galapagos Islands observing the moa and great auk."

Bambi Robbins' alibi: "The last time I saw my husband alive was at 6:10 A.M. I wrote the time next to the nighthawk on his list. Reggie had been in a foul mood, first about his fight with Donald, then because he had forgotten his notebook. But, when he found a scrap piece of paper in his bird book and I offered to write down the names of the birds he saw, he became his old darling, considerate self again. When he realized that I had left the house without gloves and a hat he sent me back to warm up."

"He must have died sometime after he sighted the starling at 6:54. I was already back at the house by then. The cook and maid will both tell you that I didn't leave again until we all went out together to look for Reggie."

Suspect 2: Lydia Robbins

Lydia Robbins, Reginald Robbins' ex-wife, was born in Coventry, England, southeast of Wolverhampton, the year that Maud and Miska Petersham won the Caldecott medal for *The Rooster Crows.*

"Reginald and I were married for 25 years," she told us. "I shared his interest in birds. I even illustrated his first book about state birds. Maybe you've seen it," she said hopefully. "I did a particularly nice job with Utah's state bird, the seagull, and with the scissor-tailed flycatcher, which is the state bird of Oklahoma."

"We were very happy until that avaricious little Bambi creature came along," Lydia Robbins sniffed. "But, I didn't fight the divorce. I knew Reginald would grow tired of her in time and come back to me. She's attractive in a cheap sort of way. But, she isn't very bright, and she knows absolutely nothing about birds. I knew that would be her downfall eventually."

Lydia Robbins' alibi: "I was sitting quietly in the woods observing a ruffed grouse. No one saw me, but I certainly didn't kill Reginald. Despite the humiliation I endured when he left me for Bambi, I loved that man."

Suspect 3: Donald Dimpthwaite

Donald Dimpthwaite, Reginald Robbins' research assistant, was born in Tell City, Indiana, on the banks of the Ohio River, the year that Bernard Malamud wrote *The Assistant.*

"Let, me tell you the truth about Reginald Robbins," Donald Dimpthwaite seethed. "He was a selfish, inconsiderate, lying popinjay. I did most of the research for his latest bird book, but he didn't give me any credit. And, he wasn't planning to give me any of the profits, either. That man was a world-class tightwad. Just ask Bambi about it. He begrudged her every dime she spent."

"Our fight was about Bambi," he admitted. "She gave me an affectionate little kiss to thank me for a pair of earrings I had given her as a Christmas present. Reginald made some irrational accusations. I got angry and compared him to the Australian kookaburra, which is sometimes called the laughing jackass. Then, I told him he was acting like the state bird of Minnesota. That's when he stormed out."

Donald Dimpthwaite's alibi: "I was alone in the woods, watching a downy woodpecker pecking around for insects in the bark of a pine tree. I didn't kill Reginald. I'm glad he's dead, but I didn't do it."

Suspect 4: Gregory Slimease

Gregory Slimease, a real estate developer, was born in Eureka, California, near the coast of the Pacific Ocean, the year that Walter Gropius designed the Pan-Am Building in New York City.

"I'm an old friend of Bambi's. When she told me that her husband owned five hundred acres of land, I figured it would be a great place for my Eden-on-Earth project— 2,000 high-priced condominiums clus-

tered around a miniature golf course and a shopping mall. I even tried to contact that Ieoh Ming Pei guy to draw up some architectural plans, but he never returned my calls. I offered old Reg $3 million, a free condominium, and lifetime membership in the Eden-on-Earth Health Club. Bambi loved the idea, but Reg kept talking about his birds and how much they needed to be protected from the wanton destruction of their habitat."

"Hey, I've dealt with bleeding heart bird lovers before. I lost a lot of money trying to build an Eden-on-Earth development in California because a bunch of fruitcakes had the land declared a refuge for the California condor. The California condor is a big, ugly bird that eats dead cattle carcasses. It's an eyesore, if you ask me."

"Bambi suggested that I come today and give old Reg another sales pitch. But, I never saw the old geezer. I got lost in the woods and ended up ruining my expensive leather shoes."

Gregory Slimease's alibi: "Hey, I was so lost out there in the woods I couldn't have found the old coot even if I had wanted to murder him. No one saw me. If someone had seen me, I wouldn't have been lost, would I?"

The Solution

Bambi wasn't as stupid as Lydia Robbins thought she was. She saw her husband standing at the edge of the cliff, his binoculars trained on a bird. In that moment she thought about everything that could be hers with a simple shove: $3 million, a condominium with a view of the miniature golf course, and a lifetime membership in the Eden-on-Earth Health Club. Bambi shoved.

Then, she realized that she needed an alibi. She took a path down to the base of the cliff, where she found Reginald's bird book lying next to his body. Inside the book was a piece of paper he had evidently used on a previous day to jot down a shopping list and a few bird sightings. Because the paper had been folded in half, he had written only on the bottom half of it. When she read the times on the paper she realized she'd have an alibi if she could get back to the house by 6:54.

Flipping through the bird book quickly, she wrote down a list of birds and times of sighting on the top half of the page, then replaced the paper in the bird book. She hurried back to the house. Knowing that it would appear he had sighted his last bird at 6:54, she made sure the cook knew she was in the house all morning.

Unfortunately for Bambi, Lydia was right when she said that Bambi's lack of knowledge about birds would be her downfall. All the birds that Bambi added to the list were migratory. They had all flown south for the winter, so Reginald could not have seen any of them on Christmas Day.

Information about the suspects

Suspect 1—Bambi Robbins
Paradise Valley is in the southeast corner of Nevada.

Betsy Byars won the Newbery medal for *Summer of the Swans* in 1971.

The moa and the great auk are both extinct.

Suspect 2—Lydia Robbins
Coventry, England, is southeast of Wolverhampton.

Maud and Miska Petersham won the Caldecott Medal for *The Rooster Crows* in 1946.

The seagull is the state bird of Utah.

The scissortailed flycatcher is the state bird of Oklahoma.

A ruffed grouse could be found in New England in December.

Suspect 3—Donald Dimpthwaite
Tell City, Indiana, is on the banks of the Ohio River.

Bernard Malamud wrote *The Assistant* in 1957.

The Australian kookaburra is sometimes called the laughing jackass.

The state bird of Minnesota is the common loon.

A downy woodpecker could be found in New England in December.

Suspect 4—Gregory Slimease
Eureka, California, is near the Pacific coast.

Walter Gropius designed the Pan-Am Building in New York City in 1958.

Ieoh Ming Pei, better known as I.M. Pei, is a contemporary architect.

The California condor is a large, ugly, endangered bird that feeds on dead cattle.

Additional Information

Migratory birds that would not have been seen in western Massachusetts on Christmas Day include: the bobolink, Baltimore oriole, catbird, indigo bunting, and nighthawk.

Non-migratory birds that could have been seen in western Massachusetts on Christmas Day include: the starling, ruffed grouse, and downy woodpecker.

Although the blue jay does migrate south for winter, blue jays from farther north take its place.

The Mystery of the Phoney Fossils

The Crime

The initial discovery was exciting enough. A nearly complete fossilized saurian skeleton had been found on an isolated butte in Wyoming. But, what followed set the world of paleontology on its ear. Entangled with the fossil remains were other bones that were hominid in nature.

"The dinosaur is a *corythosaurus*," John Sebastian Dripee acknowledged as he cast an educated glance across the site. "And, the other bones belong to a manlike creature." Then he put two and two together. "Dinosaur bones found at the same strata as hominid bones means…"

PREHISTORIC MAN FOUGHT DINOSAURS! That banner headline appeared in the next issue of the *National Enquirer.*

PALEONTOLOGIST DISCOVERS PROOF THAT DINOSAURS AND HUMANS LIVED AT THE SAME TIME!

It was not the way reputable scientists released their findings, but John Sebastian Dripee lost no time capitalizing on his sudden fame. He wrote a book, *Man and Beast—Together at Last,* which quickly soared to the top of the *New York Times* Best Sellers List.

Then a group of skeptical scientists at Harvard University subjected the findings to a carbon dating test. According to them, the dinosaur fight was a deliberately constructed hoax.

The Problem

Who faked the fossil evidence?

The Suspects

Suspect 1: Professor John Sebastian Dripee

Professor John Sebastian Dripee, a paleontologist, was born in Dar es Salaam, Tanzania, the same country where Mary Leakey and Louis Seymour Bazett Leakey discovered fossil remains of *Homo habilis*. John was born the year Roy Chapman Andrews died.

"I didn't do anything wrong," John Dripee said defensively. "The bones I found were those of a *corythosaurus*, which was still alive 65 million years ago. Remains of *Australopithecus afarensis*, one of the earliest humanlike creatures, has been dated to over four million years ago. Those are approximate dates, of course. No one left a note saying, 'I was here in 3,998,000 B.C.'"

"Dinosaurs lived on earth from the beginning of the Triassic Period, which was 225 million years ago, to the end of the Cretaceous Period, which was about 65 million years ago. Some scientists say dinosaurs appeared around 220 million years ago and disappeared rather abruptly about 63 million years ago," John Sebastian Dripee added. "Scientists themselves keep changing their minds about the dates. What's a couple of million years here or there when you're dealing with these kinds of numbers?"

"Anyway," he continued, "the earliest hominids appeared about four million years ago, leaving a gap of anywhere between 59 million years and 61 million years between the last dinosaurs and the first hominids. What's 61 million years compared to the 157 or 160 million years dinosaurs may have existed? That's only about 38% more time than we thought they were around. Suppose carbon-dating tests are inaccu-

rate? Suppose fewer cosmic rays hit the earth when the dinosaurs lived, so they absorbed less carbon-14 than the creatures that came afterward. If that's true, then it's possible for the dinosaurs to have existed up to the time of the early hominids. That is the conjecture on which I based my book."

"I stand by my theory," John Sebastian Dripee told us. "My book is selling better than ever now, and I'm due to appear on the *Phil Donahue Show* next week. The people in this country believe my theory, even if the scientists refuse to."

Professor John Sebstian Dripee's alibi: "I was never alone at the site long enough to fake the fossil evidence. Even if I had had the opportunity, I wouldn't have done anything like that. Great scientists respect the truth."

Suspect 2: Clarence Oldman

Clarence Oldman, a hunting guide, was born in Priest River, Idaho, on the upper tip of the state, the year that Henry Fairfield Osborn died.

"I've seen all kinds of people come and go," Clarence Oldman told us. "They used to come out here to shoot elk, the animal the Native Americans used to call 'hanuti.' Then the elk herds died out and the tourists wanted to see the old Native American burial grounds. Some come to photograph the spectacular scenery. Some come to find peace and tranquility. I don't care what they're looking for. If they're willing to pay me, I'm willing to take them up into the mountains."

"The professor was looking for fossils from the Old Stone Age, something called the Mesolithic Period. I thought, 'Fine, if the guy's looking for stones, I can show him enough stones to keep him happy for a lifetime. The one thing Wyoming's got is stones.' My daughter Sheila Mae was taken with him, and, to tell the truth, I didn't mind the idea of something coming about between them. A smart boy from back East with a college education wouldn't make a bad son-in-law if he could look up from his fossils long enough to pay her some attention."

Clarence Oldman's alibi: "How can I give you an alibi when I don't know when those bones were put there? It could have happened anytime in the last couple of million years. And, what's the big deal anyway? The professor paid me to help him find fossils, so I helped him find some fossils. His book is a big hit. Lots of people want me to guide them up into the mountains so they can find some fossils, too. The professor is hanging around looking for more prehistoric bones. Sheila Mae is helping him. Everybody's happy. I don't see a problem, except with some snotty Harvard boys who are jealous that they didn't find the bones first."

Suspect 3: Sheila Mae

Sheila Mae, Clarence's daughter, was born in Thermopolis, Wyoming, just north of the Owl Creek Mountains, the year *Rocky* won the Academy Award for best motion picture.

"Professor Dripee is totally perfect," Sheila Mae informed us with a love-struck sigh. "He's so smart and kind and handsome, and he's been absolutely everywhere, even to the Casbah in Morocco."

"I always go with them when my father guides Professor Dripee into the mountains. I can handle the horses as well as any man, and I know what to look for. The professor has taught me how to test limestone by pouring warm acetic acid on it. If it's real limestone, it bubbles and gives off carbon monoxide. And I'm real good at spotting shale, which consists almost entirely of compressed plant remains."

"I was actually the first one to spot the skeletons. At first, they just looked like rocks stacked kind of funny, but I saw them. I told the professor he should have a wife who could help him with his work just like Mary Leakey helped her husband Richard. I don't think he heard me, though. He was so excited about the discovery, he wouldn't have heard a Boeing 767 if it were landing on his head."

Sheila Mae Oldman's alibi: "I have the best alibi in the world. I wasn't alive four million years ago. Professor Dripee says that's when the bones were left there, and I believe everything the professor says. I did call the National Enquirer, because I wanted the professor to get all the credit he deserves, but I absolutely didn't do anything to those bones."

Suspect 4: Benson Cody

Benson Cody, the town's mayor, was born in Basin, Wyoming, on the Bighorn River, the year Pierre Teilhard de Chardin died.

"We've seen some real tough times here," Mayor Cody told us. "Ever since 1967, when federal regulations stopped us from shooting the bald eagles that feed on baby calves, we've watched the cattle ranching industry dry up. Then, the famous Donner Pass ski area just south of town closed down. I thought we were going to become a ghost town until Professor Dripee discovered that fossil site. Who would have thought people would be so interested in dinosaurs?"

"We've got fossils lying all over the place here, just ready for the taking. When I was a kid, I used to go horseback riding in the hills and come home with a saddlebag full of dinosaur bones. Didn't think nothing of them. My mother used to give them to the dogs so they'd have something to gnaw on. I probably still have a crate of them lying around in my attic."

"But, the professor made me see the light. We've got a gold mine in those fossils. People will be wanting to come and look around for themselves. They'll need to stay someplace, so we'll put up a few motels.

We'll need some restaurants to feed them and some local boys to provide the horses and act as guides. Maybe a museum. And, if folks can't come to town, we'll find the fossils for them, pack them up and ship them right to their addresses. It's a whole new life for this town."

Benson Cody's alibi: "Sure, I was out at that site before Professor Dripee discovered those bones. I'll bet I've ridden my horse past that site a thousand times, but I never knew those rocks were skeletons. The professor's a real clever man."

The Mystery of the Phoney Fossils

The Solution

Mayor Benson Cody wanted an economic revival in his town. Clarence Oldman wanted paying customers, and Sheila Mae wanted a husband. The way to get what they wanted was to make sure Professor Dripee got what he wanted—proof that dinosaurs and early hominids lived at the same time. Clarence knew where to find old Native American burial grounds. The mayor had a box of dinosaur fossils in his attic. After they mixed the bones together in the mountains, Sheila Mae eagerly helped the Professor find them. It didn't occur to them that the hoax would be discovered if the fossils were subjected to carbon-dating tests.

John Sebastian Dripee was not guilty of faking the fossil evidence, but he was guilty of three unscientific actions:

1. Accepting the physical evidence without question. He had found what he wanted to find, so he didn't wait for the scientific tests before he rushed into print with his book.

2. Thinking illogically. The carbon-dating test may have been inaccurate. But, if the dinosaurs who lived 65 million years ago were subjected to fewer cosmic rays, thereby throwing off the half-life measurements of carbon-14, why wouldn't the early hominids, who he claims lived at the same time, have received fewer cosmic rays, too? If the carbon-14 test was inaccurate for one set of fossils, it should also have been inaccurate for the other. If both the early hominids and the dinosaurs lived at the same time, the tests should have placed both at the same time, especially since the same people used the same testing procedure for both sets of fossils.

3. Failing to learn relevant information beyond his own discipline. He might have known a great deal about dinosaurs, but he couldn't have known much about early hominids if he mistook the bones of Native Americans, even those who might have died several hundred years ago, for the bones of the earliest forms of man.

Information about the suspects

Suspect 1—Professor John Sebastian Dripee

Dar es Salaam is the capital city of Tanzania.

Mary Leakey and Louis Seymour Bazett Leakey discovered fossil remains of *Homo habilis* in Tanzania.

Roy Chapman Andrews died in 1960.

The corythosaurus still existed about 65 million years ago.

Remains of *Australopithecus afarensis*, one of the earliest humanlike creatures, have been dated to over four million years ago.

Four million years ago would be roughly 3,998,000 B.C.

Scientific information about the time of the dinosaurs and the development of early man has changed and continues to change. Some reference books claim that dinosaurs lived from 225 million years ago to 65 million years ago. More recent information places the dinosaurs from 220 million years ago to about 63 million years ago. According to the first set of figures, dinosaurs existed for 160 million years. According to the second, they existed for 157 million years.

The earliest hominids appeared about four million years ago, leaving a gap of either 61 or 59 million years (depending on the figures that are used) between the last dinosaurs and the first hominids.

The earliest hominids appeared in Africa about four million years ago, but that doesn't mean hominids inhabited North America then. Most scientists think the first hominid inhabitants of North America arrived here between 20,000 and 40,000 years ago.

Sixty-one million years is 38 percent of 160 million years.

Suspect 2—Clarence Oldman

Priest River is on the upper tip of the state of Idaho.

Henry Fairfield Osborn died in 1935.

The Native Americans used to call the American elk "wapiti," not "hanuti."

The Old Stone Age was the Paleolithic Period, not the Mesolithic.

Suspect 3—Sheila Mae Oldman

Thermopolis, Wyoming, is just north of the Owl Creek Mountains.

Rocky won the Academy Award for best motion picture in 1976.

The Casbah is in Algiers, Algeria, not Morocco.

Scientists test rock to see if it is limestone by pouring cold, diluted hydrochloric acid on it. If it is limestone it bubbles and gives off carbon dioxide, not carbon monoxide.

Shale is compressed mud, not plant remains.

Richard Leakey was Mary Leakey's son, not her husband.

Suspect 4—Benson Cody

Basin, Wyoming, is on the Bighorn River.

Pierre Teilhard de Chardin died in 1955.

Bald eagles have been protected by federal laws in the lower 48 states since 1940 and in Alaska since 1953.

Bald eagles primarily eat fish. They are not a threat to the cattle industry.

The Donner Pass is in California, not Wyoming. Although it is now a ski resort, it was once the site of an unpalatable episode in American history.

Over time, minerals replaced the living tissue in fossils, so fossilized dinosaur bones are rock, not bones. The mayor's mother may have given the dinosaur bones to the dogs, but it is doubtful that the dogs gnawed on them.

The Mystery of the Phoney Fossils

The Mystery of the Poisoned Project

The Crime

"Hammy is dead!" The cry reverberated through the school auditorium, distracting science fair participants from their vinegar and baking soda volcanoes and ping-pong ball models of the solar system. They all recognized the voice, and everyone knew Hammy.

"She was a golden hamster," Julian Winterberry explained after he had calmed down enough to tell us about his science fair project. "I taught her to run through a maze and kept a record of the time it took her. Then, I changed her diet from lettuce and water to potato chips and Coca-Cola to see if the time it took her to run the maze would change. But, now she's dead! Look at her!"

Indeed, she was. Hammy lay still and untwitching on the floor of her cage, a perfect example of rodent rigor mortis. "I know it wasn't her diet that killed her," Julian insisted. "I subsist on potato chips and Coca-Cola, and I'm still alive."

The Problem

Who killed Hammy?

The Suspects

Suspect 1: Amelia Swellheart

Amelia Swellheart, a student, was born in Gloucester, Massachusetts, north of Boston, 40 years after the death of Robert H. Goddard.

"My science fair project is glaciers," Amelia explained pointing to a poster that was propped against her table. "Glaciers are formed when a lot of snow falls in the mountains. It freezes into ice, then flows down into the valleys. The bottom layers of a glacier move much faster than the top layers, so the surface breaks and crinkles up into crevasses. Sometimes pieces break off of glaciers and float in the ocean. The big chunks are called icebergs, and the smaller chunks are called growlers and bergy bits. About one-third of an iceberg is above water and the other two-thirds is below the water. I had a model of a glacier," Amelia pointed to a pan of water, "but, it melted before the judges got a chance to see it."

"I thought Julian was really mean to feed his hamster junk food like that. Hammy looked so hungry I wanted to give her something, but all I had in my pocket were some Gummi Bears covered with old tissue."

Amelia Swellheart's alibi: "I was wandering around looking at everyone else's projects. After my glacier melted, there weren't a lot of people at my table."

Suspect 2: Tommy Trivias

Tommy Trivias, a student, was born in Hazardville, Connecticut, near the Connecticut-Massachusetts border, 55 years after Vladimir K. Zworykin demonstrated the first practical television system.

"All of these exhibits are pretty lame," Tommy said with a derisive sneer. "Take this one right here." He pointed to an elaborate exhibit on primary colors. "She's got red, blue and yellow listed as the primary colors from which you can create all of the other colors, but she doesn't mention that this applies to paint, not to light. If you want to work with the composite color signals in television you have to know that the three primary colors are red, green and blue. Red and green light produce the color yellow. Equal amounts of red, green and blue light produce white. They don't teach you this stuff in school. That's why I prefer watching television."

"And so do a lot of other people," Tommy added. "Ninety-eight percent of the homes in the United States have at least one television set, and each of those sets is turned on an average of seven hours a day. All those people must know something."

Tommy Trivias' alibi: "I was so mad at my parents for dragging me to this dumb science fair, I was looking for someone to beat up. I had just about decided to punch Julian Winterberry in the face, but then he started howling about his dead hamster and people gathered around him. It doesn't pay to bash a guy when there are grown-ups watching."

Suspect 3: Goody Tushu

Goody Tushu, a student, was born in Long Beach, New York, which is on Long Island, the year Beverly Cleary won the Newbery Medal for *Dear Mr. Henshaw.*

"Julian and I were tied for first place before his hamster died," Goody told us. "But, if you want my considered opinion, we were tied only because I've garnered the first place award twice before and the judges were prejudiced against me."

"My project studies the effects of various herbicides on common plants," Goody explained as she led us to her table. "I've used bean plants, maple seedlings, lettuce plants and geraniums to test the efficacy of various substances. This set of plants was sprayed with salt, a non-selective herbicide that has been used since the 1850s. These over here have been sprayed with a selective commercial herbicide I bought at a garden center, and these…" she pointed to a bedraggled-looking set of plants, "I sprayed with Agent Orange, which is a weed killer that was used by the United States military during the Vietnam War to defoliate the jungle. Because the dioxin in Agent Orange may cause damage to human beings, the armed forces destroyed their supplies of it in 1977, but I'm fortunate enough to have an uncle who's a chemical engineer, so I was able to procure a small amount for my experiments. I sprayed all the plants at home before I brought them to the science fair," she assured us. "I wouldn't want potentially hazardous material to fall into the hands of children."

Goody Tushu's alibi: "I took a brief look around the auditorium to assess the other projects. Most of them were extremely pedestrian."

Suspect 4: Winslow Neatworth

Winslow Neatworth, a science teacher, was born in Plentywood, Montana, in the northeastern corner of the state, the year Herbert Hoover died.

"This is a truly unfortunate incident," Winslow Neatworth admitted as he examined the deceased. "Hamsters are rodents, you know. They're related to woodchucks and beavers and capybaras. And rats," he added with a shudder. "They're all rodents. The Bubonic Plague, which killed 25 percent of the people in Europe during the 1300s, was caused by infected fleas on rats. Fleas!" He shuddered once again. "I don't even like thinking about the wingless, blood-sucking vermin Julian's rodent might have brought into this building with him."

Winslow Neatworth's alibi: "I had called Julian Winterberry into my office to have a talk about maintaining a properly secure cage for Hammy. I did not want the rodent getting loose and spreading disease around the school. I'm afraid I kept Julian waiting for ten or fifteen minutes before I could join him. Goody Tushu followed me into the corridor to complain about the unfairness of the judges."

The Solution

Amelia Swellheart meant well. She hated to see poor little Hammy eating potato chips when he looked so hungry for green vegetables. All she had to give him was lint-encrusted Gummi Bears, but she saw lettuce and beans on Goody Tushu's table.

Unfortunately, Amelia didn't stop to read Goody's neatly lettered signs explaining the effects of the Agent Orange, with which she had sprayed the plants in her exhibit. The herbicide contains dioxin, a chemical that can be deadly to animals.

Julian was in Winslow Neatworth's office. Goody was in the hallway complaining to Mr. Neatworth about the science fair judges. No one saw Amelia pick a few leaves from Goody's plants and slip them through the bars of Hammy's cage. Hammy ate the evidence, which produced a most unfortunate effect.

Amelia didn't know that she was poisoning Hammy. After all, how could green vegetables kill a hamster who had survived all those meals of potato chips and Coca-Cola?

Information about the suspects

Suspect 1—Amelia Swellheart

Gloucester, Massachusetts, is north of Boston.

Robert H. Goddard died in 1945. Amelia was born 40 years later, in 1985.

Glaciers form when snow falls in the mountains and compresses into ice.

It is the top layers, not the bottom layers, of glaciers that move faster.

The big chunks of ice that fall off glaciers and float in the ocean are called icebergs. The smaller chunks are called growlers and bergy bits.

Only one-seventh to one-tenth of an iceberg is above water. Six-sevenths to nine-tenths of the iceberg is below the surface.

Suspect 2—Tommy Trivias

Hazardville, Connecticut, is near the Connecticut-Massachusetts border.

Vladimir K. Zworykin demonstrated the first practical television system in 1929. Tommy Trivias was born 55 years later, in 1984.

When dealing with paint pigments, the primary colors, from which all other colors can be created, are red, blue and yellow.

The composite color signals used in television broadcasting depend on the properties of light, not pigment. The three primary colors of light are red, green and blue.

Red and green light produce the color yellow. Equal amounts of red, green and blue light produce white.

Ninety-eight percent of the homes in the United States have at least one television set, and each of those sets is turned on an average of seven hours a day.

Suspect 3—Goody Tushu

Long Beach, New York, is on Long Island.

Beverly Cleary won the Newbery Medal in 1984 for *Dear Mr. Henshaw*.

Salt has been used as a non-selective herbicide since the 1850s.

U.S. armed forces used Agent Orange to defoliate the jungle during the Vietnam War.

There is concern that the dioxin in Agent Orange may have caused injury to human beings who were exposed to it.

The armed forces destroyed their supplies of Agent Orange in 1977.

Suspect 4-Winslow Neatworth

Plentywood, Montana, is in the northeastern corner of the state.

Herbert Hoover died in 1964.

Hamsters are rodents, as are woodchucks, beavers, capybaras and rats.

The Bubonic Plague, which killed twenty-five percent of the people in Europe during the 1300s, was caused by infected fleas on rats.

Fleas are wingless, blood-sucking insects.

Reference Test 1

Almanac   Atlas   Dictionary   Encyclopedia   *Guin*

Part I

What reference book would you use to find the following information?

1. The Flag of Monaco _____

2. The capital of South Dakota _____

3. How John Lennon died_____

4. George Washington's wife's name _____

5. The date of Annie Oakley's birth _____

6. The Year Mother Teresa won the Nobel Prize for Peace _____

7. The world's largest butterfly _____

8. The meaning of the word "research" _____

9. The population of Detroit, Michigan _____

10. The state bird of Arizona _____

Part II

In each of the following questions, underline the word you would look up to answer the question.

1. What is the capital city of Sweden?

2. What was E.B. White's first name?

3. Who won the Nobel Prize for Peace in 1985?

4. When did the Japanese bomb Pearl Harbor?

5. How did John Paul Jones die?

6. What is the state flower of Utah?

7. What does "illiterate" mean?

8. What is the atmosphere of Jupiter?

9. What movie won the Academy Award for best picture in 1958?

10. What did Alexander Graham Bell invent?

...swer the following questions?

_____

... for Peace in 1975? _____

...refer... capital of Wyoming? _____

1. How is the French flag? _____

...is the distance between Baltimore and New York? _____

6. What does "lassitude" mean? _____

7. What is the smallest fish in the world? _____

8. When did the dinosaurs become extinct? _____

9. What books did Maurice Sendak write? _____

10. What is the population of Los Angeles, California? _____

Part II

In each of the following questions, underline the word you would look up to answer the question.

1. What does "humane" mean?

2. What is the temperature on Saturn?

3. When did Martin Luther King, Jr. die?

4. How many legs does an insect have?

5. What is the state bird of Montana?

6. What is the capital of Louisiana?

7. Who painted the Mona Lisa?

8. Who won the Nobel Prize for Peace in 1963?

9. In what year did George Washington become the first president of the United States?

10. What causes pneumonia?

Answers to Reference Tests 1 & 2

Reference Test 1
Part I

1. Almanac, atlas, or encyclopedia
2. Almanac, atlas, or encyclopedia
3. Encyclopedia
4. Encyclopedia or almanac
5. Encyclopedia
6. Encyclopedia or almanac
7. *Guinness Book of World Records*
8. Dictionary
9. Atlas or almanac

Part II

1. Sweden
2. White
3. Nobel
4. Pearl
5. Jones
6. Utah
7. Illiterate
8. Jupiter
9. Academy
10. Bell

Reference Test 2
Part I

1. Encyclopedia
2. Almanac
3. Atlas, almanac, or encyclopedia
4. Almanac, encyclopedia, or atlas
5. Atlas
6. Dictionary
7. *Guinness Book of World Records*
8. Encyclopedia
9. Encyclopedia
10. Atlas or almanac

Part II

1. Humane
2. Saturn
3. King
4. Insect
5. Montana
6. Louisiana
7. Mona
8. Nobel
9. Washington
10. Pneumonia